Harcourt School Publishers

Social Studies in Action

Resources for the Classroom

Ancient Civilizations

Harcourt
SCHOOL PUBLISHERS

Orlando   Austin   New York   San Diego   Toronto   London

Visit *The Learning Site!*
www.harcourtschool.com

Contents

Unit 4

Unit 5

Unit 6

Introduction

This *Social Studies in Action: Resources for the Classroom* booklet provides a variety of activities designed to enhance students' understanding of events and issues throughout history. Some activities require students to take part in a historical event, while others allow students to write creatively on important social issues. Planning options are available in the back of the booklet. The following kinds of activities are included.

Bag Ladies Activity   These classroom activities are mini workshops. Using simple household items, students review each unit by creating fun works of art.

Drama Activity   The classroom becomes a theater for this variety of reading activities. Drama activities include original plays written about scenarios in history and various adaptations.

Simulations and Games   Games allow students to review important material in a fun but challenging way. Simulations place students directly in a historical situation and ask them to take sides, make decisions, and resolve conflicts.

Long-Term Project   The main idea of each unit is the focus of these four-week-long projects designed to integrate social studies and art.

Short-Term Projects   These projects are short and simple activities. Students explore different aspects of a unit through activities such as singing songs, drawing pictures, and making models.

Writing Projects   The main purpose of these projects is to provide writing practice. Unit content is used to facilitate various types of writing, from short stories to newspaper articles.

Daily Geography   This section provides a daily review of important concepts in geography.

Why Character Counts   These activities focus on a different character trait for each unit. Students read about and define each trait and complete an activity to reinforce understanding.

Economic Literacy   Students learn about important economic concepts related to each unit and complete an activity on sound economic principles.

Citizenship   This feature is divided into three sections. Students learn citizenship skills by reading, participating in a debate, and completing writing activities.

Film Frames
Unit 1

Materials needed:
*Permanent markers

*Overhead transparency

*Tape

*Sheet of drawing paper

*Black fine-tip marker

*Scissors

Social Studies Skills:
*Europe

*Asia and the Pacific

*Africa

*North and South America

Reading Skills:
*Compare and Contrast

*Summarize

*Sequence

Instructions:

1. On the drawing paper, create your own "film frames" similar to the examples shown. Your teacher will help you get started.

2. Write and illustrate facts about early people in the film frames on each page. (USE PENCIL AND DO NOT COLOR.)

Illustrations:

3. The teacher photocopies each completed page onto a transparency. Cut out the strips on the transparency and tape them end-to-end to create a long filmstrip.

4. Using permanent markers, color in your drawings on the BACK of the transparency.

5. Be prepared to present your project to the class on an overhead projector.

© Harcourt

Drama ACTIVITY

PIZZA STUDY

A middle school class has just studied early human life and civilization. To help prepare for the unit test, a study group meets at a local pizza parlor. How well do the students remember what they've learned? Read on to find out.

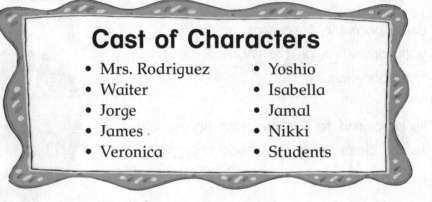

Cast of Characters

- Mrs. Rodriguez
- Waiter
- Jorge
- James
- Veronica
- Yoshio
- Isabella
- Jamal
- Nikki
- Students

[*A group of students sits around two tables at a pizza parlor. Mrs. Rodriguez, a chaperone, sits among them.*]

MRS. RODRIGUEZ:	Remember, boys and girls, we are here to study. If I knock on the table like this, (*gently raps table*) it means you are off-topic or getting too loud.
WAITER:	(*approaches table*) How is everyone this evening?
STUDENTS:	Fine.
WAITER:	(*noticing the number of notebooks on the table*) Are you all studying for a test or something?
MRS. RODRIGUEZ:	That's right. And there's nothing like a pizza party to stimulate the brain.
WAITER:	I see. So what can I bring to excite these young minds?
MRS. RODRIGUEZ:	Two large cheese pizzas and two pitchers of ginger ale ought to do it.
WAITER:	Great. That will take just long enough for you to get a head start on your study session. What are you studying anyway?
JORGE:	The birth of civilization.
NIKKI:	And life before civilization, too.
WAITER:	Oh, you mean the Paleolithic era?
NIKKI:	Yeah, before there were written records.
WAITER:	Well, study away. I'll have your drinks out shortly. (*hurries away to another table*)

© Harcourt

MRS. RODRIGUEZ:	All right, let's talk about prehistory. Who can tell me where archaeologists found fossils of early hominids?
YOSHIO:	In Eastern Africa. One of these groups was called the australopithecines. Some of them lived in forests, and some lived in grasslands.
JAMES:	Wow, Yoshio. It sounds like you actually read the book.
MRS. RODRIGUEZ:	I hope the same is true for you, James. The unit test is less than a week away.
JAMES:	I was just kidding. Ask me anything.
MRS. RODRIGUEZ:	Which hominid was the first known toolmaker?
JAMES:	*Homo…um…erectus?*
NIKKI:	No, James. It's *Homo habilis. Homo erectus* came later. *Homo erectus* made better tools and mastered the use of fire.
MRS. RODRIGUEZ:	Good job, Nikki. Now who can tell me about the group called *Homo sapiens?*
ISABELLA:	*Homo sapiens* were the first modern humans, and they appeared 200,000 years ago. They had better tools, weapons, and language.
MRS. RODRIGUEZ:	And why was this hominid so advanced?
NIKKI:	I know! They had larger brains. *Homo sapiens* means "wise person," right?
MRS. RODRIGUEZ:	That's right. So how did these wise people survive?
JAMAL:	(*leans over to Yoshio*) I think it was by hunting and gathering food.
YOSHIO:	Right. Farming didn't happen until the agricultural revolution. During the Ice Age, hunting and gathering was the way of life.
WAITER:	(*places two pitchers of ginger ale on the table*) Here you go.
MRS. RODRIGUEZ:	Can anybody say "thank you"?
STUDENTS:	Thank you!

MRS. RODRIGUEZ:	You might remember reading that early people migrated to different continents. Does anyone remember how people traveled to other continents?
YOSHIO:	During the Ice Age, glaciers caused ocean levels to drop. Then, land bridges between continents became uncovered, and people crossed over them.
JORGE:	And when early humans migrated to Europe, they saw the Neanderthals and the Cro-Magnons.
JAMAL:	I just read that in my notes. Neanderthals buried their dead and Cro-Magnons created the first known art.
MRS. RODRIGUEZ:	Remember, all of these early people adapted to their environments, which means what?
ISABELLA:	That means they had to change according to their surroundings.
YOSHIO:	Right. And when the Ice Age ended, people began to form societies and follow rules.
ISABELLA:	But they were still nomads, right?
YOSHIO:	Yes, but as Earth became warmer, people became more settled. Plants and small animals were more plentiful.
VERONICA:	(approaches the table and takes a seat) Hey, everybody. Sorry I'm late.
STUDENTS:	Hi, Veronica.
MRS. RODRIGUEZ:	We're still on the first chapter, Veronica.
VERONICA:	Great, I was just studying at the dentist's office. Ask me anything!
JORGE:	What was the name of one of the first settlements along the Euphrates…
VERONICA:	Abu Hureyra!
JORGE:	You didn't even let me finish.
VERONICA:	Sorry, I guess I got a little excited.
JAMES:	How can you get excited about social studies?
YOSHIO:	What could be more exciting than discussing the history of humankind?
JAMES:	Eating pizza!
NIKKI:	Is food all you think about, James?
MRS. RODRIGUEZ:	(raps the table gently with her fist) Alright, let's continue studying. I promise that everyone will benefit from learning this material.
ISABELLA:	Are we going to talk about North America?
MRS. RODRIGUEZ:	Good idea, Isabella. What do you remember about the Clovis people?

© Harcourt

ISABELLA:	They were one of the first cultures in North America. They came from New Mexico, and they made special spear points. They used the spear points to hunt large Ice Age animals. But they died out when these animals began to disappear.
MRS. RODRIGUEZ:	Well, somebody has been reading up on North America!
JAMAL:	What about South America?
JAMES:	There is some important site there called Monte…(*hesitates*)
JAMAL:	I believe it's called Monte Verde.
MRS. RODRIGUEZ:	That's correct. And why is this an important site?
JORGE:	It shows that people may have settled in the Americas more than 12,000 years ago.
VERONICA:	Are we going to talk about the agricultural revolution?
JAMES:	We haven't gotten that far yet.
MRS. RODRIGUEZ:	Since you brought it up, Veronica, why did people start farming?
VERONICA:	Droughts caused food shortages. Also, populations were increasing. People were looking for ways to survive.
YOSHIO:	Farming was more difficult than hunting and gathering. Land had to be cleared and livestock had to be cared for.
JAMAL:	And livestock are domesticated animals that provide resources.
JAMES:	Can we take a break between chapters?
MRS. RODRIGUEZ:	James, we haven't heard many answers from you yet. Perhaps you can explain what *domestication* means.
JAMES:	That's easy. It means taming animals. People did that when they started farming.
NIKKI:	Is that the one thing you studied, James?
JAMES:	(*smiling*) I've studied both chapters. I'm going to ace this test.
WAITER:	Who's hungry? (*places two large pizzas in the middle of the table*)
JAMAL:	I could eat a whole pizza by myself!
MRS. RODRIGUEZ:	All right, everybody put your notebooks under the tables for now. We'll practice vocabulary from memory while we eat. Let's see… what was slash-and-burn farming?
JAMES:	(*slides down in his seat*) Uh-oh.
NIKKI:	I think James just volunteered!

THE END

UNIT 1

Simulations and Games

EXCAVATION The object of this game is to "uncover" important terms by deciphering clues about a term. Divide students into three equal groups. Tell each group to pick five terms and write three clues about each term. The first clue should be a general one. The second and third clues should be more descriptive. Each team takes turns offering clues to the other two teams. Each time a clue is used, it should be recorded. The teams must try to guess terms using as few clues as possible. After all terms have been "uncovered," the team that used the least amount of clues wins. *GAME*

TIC-TAC-TOE WITH A TWIST This is a twist on an old classic. Divide the class into two teams. Ask each team to devise a list of ten to fifteen questions, depending on the time allotted. The questions should be based on material found in the unit. The questions should start simply and get increasingly difficult. Quickly review each team's questions to ensure fair play, and then draw a giant tic-tac-toe grid on the board. Flip a coin to determine which team goes first. Each team should appoint one person

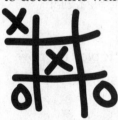

to read the questions as needed. A team must answer a question correctly to be able to put an *X* or *O* on the board. No student may answer a question twice. This should encourage as many students to participate as possible. Play until a team wins. *GAME*

WORD SCRAMBLE This game will test how well students know important terms from the unit. On the board, write scrambled versions of selected vocabulary words from the unit. Students will use their own paper to try to unscramble the words as quickly as possible. Students should not use their textbooks to figure out the words. The first student to correctly unscramble all the words, or the most words within a specified time period, wins. *GAME*

EXCAVATION BINGO Ask students to get out sheets of paper and draw grids like the ones archaeologists use when excavating a site. Grids should be five rows of five squares each. Students should number the squares from 1 to 25 in any order they wish (these grids will be their bingo cards). Write the numbers 1 through 25 on a sheet of paper and tear the paper into small squares so that only one number appears on each piece of paper. Put the pieces of paper in a bag, box, or other container where the numbers cannot be seen. Draw one number at a time until a student has bingo across, down, or diagonally. Before you reveal each number, ask the class a question pertaining to the unit. Try to review archaeology as much as possible. *GAME*

B	I	N	G	O
1	6	11	16	21
2	7	12	17	22
3	8	13	18	23
4	9	14	19	24
5	10	15	20	25

EARLY TOWNS In this simulation, students will get a chance to play a part in an early town and in the development of early trade agreements. Divide the class into the two towns of Jericho and Çatal Hüyük. Each town must determine its method of leadership. Then the two towns must make a trade agreement. For example, Jericho may want to obtain some obsidian from Çatal Hüyük, and Çatal Hüyük may want a particular crop from Jericho. Consider specifics of how the agreement would have likely come together around 6500 B.C. Remember that Çatal Hüyük controlled the obsidian trade at the time, and both towns were capable of producing surplus crops because of their location near water. Have each town draft a proposal that includes how the goods will be exchanged. Have members of the town meet until an agreement can be reached. *SIMULATION*

Long-Term Project

EARLY WORLD'S FAIR

Early civilizations developed all over the world. As societies became more complex, there were many more choices to be made. For example, if a society had a food surplus, members could work in trades other than agriculture. Students will create an Early World's Fair to show how different communities developed into more complex societies.

Week 1

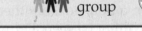 group   45 minutes

Materials: paper, pens, resource materials

Explain to the class that they will take part in creating an Early World's Fair. Divide students into the following regions: Africa, Europe, Asia and the Pacific, North America, and South America. Tell groups that they are responsible for a booth to represent their regions at the fair. The booth should include the following things: a colorful poster that includes a map showing the location of the region, samples of products from the region, a diagram of the government of the region, and anything else that will give other students a sense of the region. Allow students to brainstorm what their booths will look like.

To guide students further, tell them that they must answer the following questions. Encourage them to make up their own questions as well.

    Question 1: What type of government did your region have?

    Question 2: What was the major product of your region?

    Question 3: Was there something for which your region was particularly known?

    Question 4: Was there a system of trade in your region?

Week 2

group   45 minutes

Materials: paper, pencils, resource materials

This week, students should focus on the research necessary to design their booths and answer the questions posed in Week 1. Groups should already know to which area each person is assigned and should spend this session looking for answers to their questions. Circulate among the students to make sure that they are finding the information they need from the appropriate sources.

Week 3

👥 group   🕐 45 minutes

Materials: posterboard, glue, markers, decorations for booths

Have groups assemble their booths this week. Information should be clearly and attractively displayed, and each region should be distinctive. Students should be encouraged to bring product samples or replicas of early tools and pottery. Depending on the information each group was able to find, students may also include samples of a region's jewelry or other items that show what a region was like.

Week 4

👥 group   🕐 45 minutes

Materials: any items needed to finish the booths

The fair should begin with a person from each group giving a short overview of the appropriate region. Students should be encouraged to tell how they found their information, and anything that is not too delicate should be passed around during the presentation. After all of the regions have been presented, students should spend time at each of the other booths to get a flavor of ancient civilizations from around the world.

Tips for combination classrooms:

5-6 For grade five, have students participate in the fair by assigning regions of the United States. Have students answer the same basic questions as the students in grade six.

6-7 For grade seven, discuss early scientific and cultural developments in Rome. Have students focus on Roman contributions in the areas of architecture, law, and so on.

Short-Term Projects

Archaeologists use relics to learn about ancient times. In these activities, students explore the science of archaeology and participate in the culture of early people.

Assembling the Past   small group   40 minutes

Materials: paint or markers, 4–5 clay pots in two different sizes, paper grocery bag, hammer, glue

Students can experience a little of what it is like to be an archaeologist by doing the following activity. In a small group, have students decorate clay pots with paint or magic markers. Tell them to make each pot distinct from the others in terms of design. Put all the pots in a brown paper grocery bag. Tap the pots lightly with a hammer until the pots break into pieces. Shake the bag carefully, and then give each member of the group a handful of the broken pieces. Students should spread the pieces out in front of them and see if any of the pieces fit together. Have students glue together any pieces that appear to be from the same pot. By doing this activity, students can see what it is like to try to piece together information when parts of an object are missing.

Make a Cave Painting   individual   30 minutes

Materials: brown paper grocery bag, tempera paints (preferably brown, dark red, black), paintbrushes

The best place to do this activity is in the dark! Students can make their own cave paintings by tearing open brown paper grocery bags and then crumpling them up to make them as small as possible. Students will then smooth out the bags to make their own "cave walls." Encourage students to make paintings of animals that would have been important to life in ancient times. Tell them to mimic the style of painting that early humans used. If possible, turn off the lights—remember that there would have been no electric lighting in caves! When students have finished their cave paintings, they can display their artwork in the classroom.

Talking History

👥 partners   🕐 20 minutes

Materials: "artifacts" from the classroom

Archaeologists must construct the history of an object by carefully examining the object for clues. Ask each student to choose one item in the classroom and carry it back to his or her seat. (Students may choose a personal item if they prefer.) Have students work in pairs. Students should spend a few minutes in silence closely examining the item for clues such as dust, markings, wear and tear, etc. Then they should take turns telling each other everything they were able to deduce by looking at the item. For example, a student might say, "I think that whoever used this pencil may have been a worrier. There are teeth marks on the pencil." Challenge students to try to find at least five clues on the item they chose. Another twist to this activity would be to challenge students to explain the use of the item to their partners. They must pretend that their partners have never seen the item before and have no idea what it is used for.

Specialized Labor

👤👤👤 small group   🕐 30 minutes

Materials: modeling clay or colored pencils and paper

As towns began to have food surpluses, early people were able to do jobs other than farming. Some people became specialized laborers, making tools, jewelry, clothing, or pottery. Ask students to imagine that they are specialized laborers and they are designing their latest products. Have students make a replica of an ancient product using modeling clay. As an alternative, have students use colored pencils and paper to design and draw the product. When they have finished, ask students to share their products with a small group. They should tell the group what they made or drew and what its use would have been in ancient society.

© Harcourt

UNIT 1 Writing Projects

Ancient people changed with their environment. As Earth became warmer, people began farming and eventually formed societies. Students explore changes such as these by writing creatively.

Rules for the People

As societies became more complex, there was an increased need for leadership. More people were living in a concentrated area. People worked in trades other than agriculture. Towns bartered or traded with each other for goods or crops, and societies became divided by social class. The highest social class was usually the leaders. Ask your students to think about what makes a good civilization. They should consider systems of money, trade, and so on. Ask students to invent their own town, and have them write an essay explaining the major rules of the town. Encourage students to give careful consideration to the consequences of the rules that they devise.

Family Migration

Early humans were often on the move. A family might stay in one area for a while, but then they would have to move on to find more food. Ask students to imagine that they are members of a family that must migrate. Have students write a descriptive essay about the day they finally break camp and leave for a new place. Encourage students to use sensory details to describe their "moving day."

The Legend of the Bison

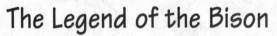

Cultures often have fables associated with them. Fables are mythical stories that usually portray an important truth. In fables, animals often talk like humans. Challenge students to write a fable. Encourage students to use their imaginations to develop a story that tells an important truth. Tell students to write the fable as if they lived in ancient times. For example, a student may write a fable titled "The Legend of the Bison." If students need inspiration, try reading the class a short fable.

© Harcourt

Trade Brochure

Invite students to make a promotional brochure for an ancient town that wants to trade with other neighboring towns. Students can use eight-by-eleven sheets of paper and make double or triple-fold brochures. The brochures should be attractive with the purpose of getting other towns to enter into trade or barter agreements. Ask students to think about what item(s) their towns may have to trade and then highlight them in a brochure. Challenge students to create a catchy slogan to write on their brochures.

Breaking News

Archaeologists often work a very long time with little or no recognition. Sometimes, however, they make an amazing discovery that captures the attention of the rest of the world. Ask students to write an imaginary newspaper article about an exciting discovery in archaeology. They should review the unit for ideas. Tell students that they must identify what the discovery was by answering the following questions in their article: Who, What, When, Where, Why, and How.

Breaking the Ice Age

Tell students that they have been hired by a textbook publisher to create a section of a middle-school textbook about the Ice Age. Allow students to use the library, classroom resources, or the Internet to explore facts about the Ice Age. Explain that the information they uncover should be both accurate and interesting, and should encourage others to want to learn about this period in history. Encourage students to write in a creative style, but remind them that the information they use must be factual.

Daily Geography

1. **Location**   On which continent have archaeologists found traces of early hominids called australopithecines?

2. **Human-Environment Interactions**   Why did some australopithecines become stronger and grow longer legs than others?

3. **Place**   Where in Africa did Mary and Louis Leakey first find *Homo habilis* bones?

4. **Place**   Where were the first discoveries of *Homo erectus* made?

5. **Human-Environment Interactions**   *Homo erectus* was the first known hominid to master the use of what?

6. **Location**   From which continent did early people most likely begin their global migration?

7. **Human-Environment Interactions**   How did early humans use the animals that they hunted?

8. **Human-Environment Interactions**   What environmental factor caused *Homo erectus* to migrate outside Africa?

9. **Movement**   During the last Ice Age, how were early humans able to get from Africa to southwestern Asia?

10. **Location**   After the last Ice Age, which desert in Africa received enough rain to foster plant life?

11. **Place**   Where in southern Africa did early people set up camp about 15,000 years ago?

12. **Place**   People living along which European sea devised tools for catching fish?

13. **Place**   What was the name of one of the world's first settlements along the Euphrates River in Syria?

© Harcourt

14. Regions   Archaeologists first found Clovis points in which region of North America?

15. Place   What important archaeological site can be found in southern Chile?

16. Place   Which mountain range in South America stretches more than 4,500 miles?

17. Regions   The world's first farmers came from which part of the world?
South America   Asia
Africa   Australia

18. Human-Environment Interactions   Which kind of farming was practiced in areas where there were thick forests?

19. Place   Which farming village in southwestern Asia contained more than 25 houses by 7000 B.C.?

20. Region   By 5500 B.C., the *Bandkeramik* people had established farming communities in which region?
Europe   Asia
Africa   North America

21. Place   By 5000 B.C., which community in Asia had begun to grow cotton to weave into cloth?

22. Location   In which part of the world did the Yangshao culture build their village on terraces?

23. Location   In which continent is the Nile River located?

24. Regions   In which part of the world was irrigation first developed?

25. Place   Which farming village controlled the trade of obsidian?

26. Place   Which settlement in southwestern Asia was protected by a huge wall?

27. Movement   Traders heading east from Jericho would cross which desert?

28. Location   Which sea borders both Asia and Africa?

29. Regions   Which region of the world was the birthplace of the first cities?

30. Place   What were the names of four of the world's first cities?

© Harcourt

Why Character Counts

- **Trustworthiness**
- # Respect
- **Responsibility**
- **Fairness**
- **Caring**
- **Patriotism**

Respect

One of the most basic building blocks of any civilization is respect. Without it, a civilization cannot survive.

When you have respect for someone, it means that you show consideration or regard for a person's feelings, beliefs, values, or morals. For example, people in a courtroom show respect for the judge by standing when he or she enters the courtroom. Respect is also an attitude of admiration or esteem for a person or an idea.

Ancient civilizations were founded on the idea of respect. People had to respect nature, animal life, and each other as they struggled to survive in new and sometimes harsh environments.

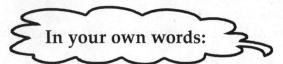

In your own words:

Write a definition for the word *respect*.

_____

_____

_____

_____

Character Activity

Imagine a difficult situation where two people must show respect to one another even though they disagree. Write a short scene of dialogue between two characters who are in the middle of a disagreement but who still show respect for one another. Make sure you identify what the disagreement is about in your dialogue.

_____

_____

_____

_____

_____

_____

_____

_____

_____

_____

_____

_____

_____

_____

_____

_____

Economic Literacy

Surplus

Have you ever heard the term *surplus*? It's a fancy way of saying *extra*. Have you ever had more than you needed of something? If so, that can be considered a surplus. For example, let's say your softball team held a fundraiser to get money for new equipment. The fundraiser went so well that after the team purchased all the new equipment, there was still money left over. That is a surplus. Your team must then decide how to use the surplus. It could save the money, buy extra team uniforms, or give the money to charity.

Ancient people found that once they had mastered farming, they could try to grow enough crops to produce a surplus. They found that there were many benefits to growing enough crops to yield an extra supply of seeds. Farmers had many choices about how to use this surplus. Some used the seeds to plant for the next season. Some farmers decided to store the seeds to use as food when crops were more difficult to grow. Others lent their extra seeds to settlements that were struggling.

When you have a surplus, you have the ability to make choices. For example, if you have an allowance or some spending money, you may be able to find a way to produce your own surplus.

© Harcourt

Surplus Activity

Imagine that you receive an allowance of $10 a week. You are responsible for buying any school supplies you might need, and you must put at least $1 per week into savings. The rest of the money can be spent however you wish. At the end of the month, you have a surplus of $6. You must choose what to do with it. Will you spend it at the mall? Will you buy pizza with it? Will you save it? Will you invest in some extra school supplies?

On the lines below, write what you will do with your surplus money. First, write down what all of your options are for using the money. Then, explain why you think your choice is better than the other choices you could have made.

_____

_____

_____

_____

_____

_____

_____

_____

_____

_____

_____

_____

_____

_____

_____

Citizenship

Read About It   The concept of government has been around for thousands of years. Today, we define government as the unit of our society that has the authority to make and enforce laws. But it is more than just a law-making body. The government controls taxation and makes decisions that are critical for the common good. In ancient civilizations, the very earliest form of government appeared with the division of labor. As social classes emerged, the highest class was usually made up of leaders from powerful families. At first, the power stayed within the families and was passed on to other family members over the years. As towns and cities became more and more complex, a need arose for even more organized forms of leadership.

1. In what ways were the earliest forms of government like our government today?

    _____

    _____

    _____

    _____

2. In what ways were they different?

    _____

    _____

    _____

    _____

Talk About It   What is your impression of the purpose of government? Is it good, bad, or somewhere in between? What role should government play in our lives? Give support for your opinions as you share your feelings with classmates. Listen carefully to your classmates' opinions, and make only constructive comments.

© Harcourt

Name _____

Write About It Do you think that people in government have a greater responsibility than the average citizen? Should more be expected of someone in a public position? Why or why not? What do you expect from an elected official in the government? Write an essay in which you answer these questions. Make sure to support your opinions with examples.

_____
_____
_____
_____
_____
_____
_____
_____
_____
_____
_____
_____
_____
_____
_____
_____

© Harcourt

Travel Ticket
Unit 2

Materials needed:

*Sheet of drawing paper

*Tape

*Scissors

*Sheet of construction paper
cut to $8\frac{1}{2}''$ square

*Markers, crayons, or colored
pencils

Instructions:

1. Fold the drawing paper into
   thirds and cut along the folds.
   Create three travel tickets
   similar to the example shown. On
   the departure lines, write *Sumer*,
   Egypt, and *Nubia*. Fill out the
   information as you travel from
   Sumer to *Egypt* and finally to
   Nubia.

2. Write information about the land,
   the past, and the culture of each
   area.

Social Studies Skills:

*Egypt

*Sumer

*Nubia

Reading Skills:

*Compare and Contrast

*Sequence

*Generalize

Illustrations:

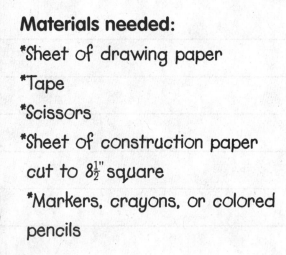

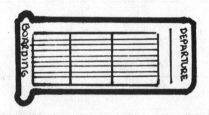

© Harcourt

3. Fold the construction paper in half to make a holder for the tickets. Tape it across the bottom and $\frac{3}{4}$ of the way up the open side.

4. Fold the top sheet of the paper on a diagonal from the top of the tape to the top corner. Tuck the triangle inside. Decorate the outside of the ticket holder.

TAPE

MY AIRLINE

FLY MY STYLE

Departure to:
EGYPT

UNIT 2
SUMER, EGYPT AND NUBIA

FLY MY STYLE

Departure to:
EGYPT

UNIT 2
SUMER, EGYPT AND NUBIA

INTERPRETING HAMMURABI'S CODE

A middle school social studies class has just finished studying Hammurabi's Code. Some of the students are doing a project for extra credit. They are interpreting and discussing a few of Hammurabi's laws. Later, they will give a presentation to the class. Join in to discuss Hammurabi's brand of justice, including the idea of "an eye for an eye."

Cast of Characters

- Mr. Adell
- Sara
- Yolanda
- Kevin
- Marcus

[Four students sit in a circle in a classroom after school. Mr. Adell, the social studies teacher, is working at his desk, but often joins the conversation with the students. The students have notebooks and pens on their desks. A book open to a list of Hammurabi's laws sits on a nearby table.]

MR. ADELL: (*straightening papers on his desk*) OK, boys and girls, I'm going to grade these quizzes from today. If you have any questions, feel free to shout them out.

KEVIN: I guess we'd better get started. I have soccer practice at 4:00.

SARA: OK, let's take a look at some of these laws. Marcus, the book is closest to you. Can you read them?

MARCUS: Yeah, sure. (*picks up the book next to him and looks puzzled*) Which one?

SARA: Well, there can't be that many. This was ancient times. How much could there have been to make laws about?

KEVIN: Come on. We're wasting time.

MARCUS: (*smiling*) Well, it's going to take a while to read all these. (*flipping a few pages in the book*) It looks like there were 282 laws.

YOLANDA: Mr. Adell, you tricked us! We can never interpret all these laws!

MR. ADELL: (*looking up from his desk*) I didn't ask you to talk about all of them in your presentation. I just want your classmates to get a sense of what the language was like and how serious Hammurabi was when he organized those laws. Anyway, look more closely, Marcus, and you'll see that the text for laws 66–99 is missing.

© Harcourt

MARCUS:	Hey, you're right. What happened to them?
MR. ADELL:	Well, when the laws were discovered, laws 66–99 were missing from the stone slab.
YOLANDA:	You mean 282 laws were written in stone? That must have taken a while.
MR. ADELL:	Not only were they written in stone, but they were also set in a public place where everyone could see them. No one could say that he or she didn't know what the law was.
KEVIN:	Where are the laws now, by the way? Can people see them?
MR. ADELL:	You sure can, but you'll need an expensive plane ticket. The stone is in the Louvre in Paris, France.
SARA:	Field trip!
KEVIN:	We'd better get going on this. We're going to run out of time.
MARCUS:	OK, here goes. (*reading from the book*) Law 2 says, "If any one bring an accusation against a man, and the accused go to the river and leap into the river, if he sink in the river his accuser shall take possession of his house. But if the river prove that the accused is not guilty, and he escape unhurt, then he who had brought the accusation shall be put to death, while he who leaped into the river shall take possession of the house that had belonged to his accuser."
SARA:	You must be kidding. Isn't there a shorter one?
KEVIN:	No, wait. I think I get it—except for the part about jumping in the river. It sounds like Hammurabi wanted to make absolutely sure someone was guilty before he was punished.
YOLANDA:	I think it sounds like he wanted to keep people from randomly accusing one another. If you couldn't prove your accusation, you got put to death. That doesn't sound fair.
MARCUS:	Right. There are plenty of times you know someone is guilty but you can't prove it. It happens all the time today. I'd be afraid to accuse anyone of anything in Hammurabi's day.
MR. ADELL:	I think that was Hammurabi's point in a way. He wanted to use the laws to protect people, but he didn't want people to be able to take advantage of one another.
KEVIN:	But what does jumping in the river prove? What if the guy couldn't swim? How fair is that?

© Harcourt

MR. ADELL:	Well, at the time it was thought that a guilty man would sink to the bottom. So in Hammurabi's mind, it was a way of positively proving someone's guilt or innocence.
SARA:	That's just crazy. And how can you lose your house over something like that?
MR. ADELL:	I know it sounds a little different because we don't do things like that today in the United States, but it's not really fair to call it crazy. They were completely different times. Why don't you try to find another law and see how it compares to this one? See if you think all the laws were that harsh.
KEVIN:	Yeah, Marcus, read another one.
MARCUS:	OK, let me see . . . (looking through the pages) How about Law 196? It says, "If a man put out the eye of another man, his eye shall be put out." And 197 says, "If he break another man's bone, his bone shall be broken."
SARA:	Wait, we read something about that in our books. What was that called? Equal rights? (grabs her history book and starts thumbing through the pages)
MARCUS:	No, that wasn't it. It was something else. Mr. Adell, what was it?
MR. ADELL:	I think what you're all thinking of is the idea of equal justice. It was very important to Hammurabi.
SARA:	(still looking down at her book) But it says here that equal justice only went so far. The entire society was still divided into social classes.
MR. ADELL:	That's true. Hammurabi believed in equal justice within a social class. So as you look through the laws, you'll see that they're different depending on whether you were a free man or a slave.
YOLANDA:	Then that's not equal.
KEVIN:	I agree. How can you treat one person one way and another a different way and call that equal?
MARCUS:	Law 198 says, "If he put out the eye of a freed man, or break the bone of a freed man, he shall pay one gold mina." Then 199 says, "If he put out the eye of a man's slave, or break the bone of a man's slave, he shall pay one-half of its value."
MR. ADELL:	That's a good example of what I mean. Your punishment would be decided based on your level in society.

YOLANDA:	I still say it's not equal. Equal means everyone gets treated the same.
SARA:	But even today when we're all supposed to be equal, we know some people are treated better or worse than others.
KEVIN:	That's true, but unlike Hammurabi's Code, the laws of the United States say that everyone is equal. Hammurabi's laws said that people were different because of social class. That's a big difference.
MR. ADELL:	That's a good point, Kevin. One thing Hammurabi wanted to accomplish by compiling his laws was to keep the stronger people from taking advantage of the weaker people. This way, if a free man wronged a slave, there was still some penalty.
YOLANDA:	Marcus, pass the book over here. I want to take a look at these so-called equal laws. (*reaches out for the text*)
MR. ADELL:	Let me mention one other thing to help you understand. Does anyone remember what Hammurabi's position was?
MARCUS:	He was Emperor of the Babylonian Empire, right?
MR. ADELL:	Right. Originally, Hammurabi was the king of the city-state of Babylon. Then he conquered most of Mesopotamia and formed his empire. But before that, each city-state had its own laws.
KEVIN:	Oh, so Hammurabi made just one set?
MR. ADELL:	He did. But first he collected all the laws from the city-states and studied them. Then he wrote the single collection you're reading here today.
KEVIN:	That must have taken a long time. What were the laws like before?
MR. ADELL:	Well, at times they were very confusing and unfair. The way Hammurabi explained the laws was very clear. So just keep that in mind.
KEVIN:	It's almost time for soccer. I guess we'd better get together again to finish this up.
SARA:	(*starting to pack up her things*) Yeah, I guess we'd better.
MR. ADELL:	You all have done a good job today. Now get out of here and have some fun. These quizzes still aren't graded!

THE END

UNIT 2 Simulations and Games

MAKE YOUR OWN WORD SEARCH   To play this game students will need graph paper and pencils. Write the following words on the board: TIGRIS, UBAID, KISH, SUMER, CARAVAN, ZIGGURAT, SCRIBES, EMPIRE, SARGON, DELTA, AFTERLIFE, GIZA, DYNASTY, VIZIER, PAPYRUS, MUMMY, NUBIA, PHARAOH, KERMA, and ANNEX. Tell students that they will each be making a word search game. Students should draw a box of 15 x 15 squares on the graph paper. They should then write the words for the word search game on the grid. Set ground rules that determine how words can be listed (i.e. diagonally, horizontally, vertically, and reversed). Students should fill in all the empty boxes with other letters from the alphabet. All letters should be uppercase. Once students have completed their word searches, they should trade with classmates and play the game. As they play, invite students to the board to define the words. The first student to hand in a completed word search wins. However, all words must be defined before any word searches are handed in. *GAME*

WHO RULES THE SPELLING DYNASTY?   The purpose of this game is to review vocabulary and enhance spelling skills. Prior to playing the game with the class, make up a list of vocabulary words, place names, and the names of rulers. Divide students into two teams and have them sit on opposite sides of the room. Tell students that a correct answer is worth a point, but an incorrect answer will cost a point. Say a word such as *Khartoum*, and allow the student who raises his or her hand first to try to spell the word. If the student spells the word correctly, that team gets a point. Give the student the option of defining the word for an extra point, with no penalty for a wrong answer. If the student spells the word incorrectly, someone from the opposite team should be given the chance to spell the word. Keep score on the board. Make sure that you intersperse easier terms such as import, with harder terms such as Eridu. Encourage all team members to join in. *GAME*

1. Khartoum

2. silt

3. Nubia

4. import

ADD A FACT! This game will test students' knowledge of different parts of the unit. Divide students into two groups. Say a word such as *Egypt* to the first group. The group must come up with one accurate fact about Egypt. Then the second group must add a fact about Egypt. Play continues until one of the groups does not have a fact to add. The point goes to the last team to give a fact. You can decide if there is a penalty for incorrect facts. Try to use words about which more than one thing can be said, such as mummies, tombs, trade, writing, dynasties, Tigris, Sumer, and so on. The team with the most points at the end of a specified time wins. *GAME*

FORMS OF LEADERSHIP In this simulation students will debate a proposed change in the form of leadership for a city-state. Sumerian city-states each had their own form of government. Often a small group of leaders ruled a city-state. There was a chief leader, but all the leaders played a role in the decision-making process. As time went on, the form of leadership shifted to a monarchy. Divide the class into two groups. Ask students to imagine they are members of the old leadership in a city-state engaging in a simple debate. One group should support the change from the old government to a monarchy, and the other group should be against the change. Have each side present its argument. Remind students that their arguments need to be historically based. Students should consider likely reasons a Sumerian leader would be for or against such a change. Remind students that current models of government do not apply here. *SIMULATION*

2 Long-Term Project

EGYPTIAN ART EXHIBITION

One of the most important and fascinating aspects of a civilization is its artwork. The artwork of Egypt shows how important the afterlife was and what things Egyptians valued the most. In this project, students will get a chance to study and recreate the artwork of Egypt.

Week 1 　　　　　　　　　🧍🧍🧍 group　🕛 45 minutes

Materials: paper, pencils, resource materials

Introduce the project by asking questions such as the following: What is art? What makes good art? Is there such a thing as bad art? Can you think of an artist you admire and why? What does art say about culture and society?

Introduce the topic of the artwork of Egypt and remind students that, especially in ancient times, art showed what was valuable to a society. Explain to the class that they will have a chance to study different aspects of art from ancient Egypt. Then each group will attempt a recreation of Egyptian art to be displayed in Week 4. Each group will also give a short oral presentation during Week 4. Break the class into at least four groups. Assign each group a particular type of art from Egypt. For example, the four groups could be statuettes (both human and animal), paintings, funeral masks and coffins, and relief sculptures.

To guide students further, tell them that the oral presentations should address the following questions:

1. What type of art did you investigate?
2. What materials were used in creating the art?
3. Where in Egypt was the art typically found?
4. What Egyptian characteristics are present in the artwork?
5. In what way was the art important?

In the first week, students should brainstorm about how to approach their research. As soon as possible, students should make a list of materials they will need to do their artwork. Remind students that they will need to be creative. They may not be able to produce a stone or wood sculpture, but they should be able to find materials to create a reasonable facsimile.

© Harcourt

Week 2

👥 group 🕐 45 minutes

Materials: paper, pencils, resource materials

This week students should focus on the research necessary to answer the questions posed in Week 1. Students should already know what task or item each person has been assigned and should spend the time this week looking for answers to their questions. Circulate among the students to make sure that they are finding the information they need from the appropriate sources. If they have not already done so, students should make a list of materials they will need to complete their replicas.

Week 3

👥 group 🕐 45 minutes

Materials: art materials (will vary according to group)

Students should create their artwork this week. Materials should be acquired from the art department or brought in from home. Students should attempt to faithfully recreate the object they have chosen. Students making a relief, for example, may try working with slabs of clay. The art should be a team effort.

Week 4

👥 group 🕐 45 minutes

Materials: any art materials needed to finish the replica

Students should take a short time to finish their artwork if needed. After the artwork is complete, display it in a safe place in the classroom. Have each group present its art and give oral presentations. Ask students to share what they found most interesting about the project over the last four weeks.

Tips for combination classrooms:

 For grade five, have students research different forms of art in the United States. Students can make a replica of the art form they have studied.

 For grade seven, have students research art forms from Rome, China, or Japan. Students should make a replica of the art form they have studied.

Short-Term Projects

In ancient Egypt, new and wonderful marvels appeared. These projects will give students a chance to construct pyramids, make cuneiform tablets, and do other activities that will enhance their understanding of ancient times.

Building Pyramids   👥 partners   🕐 40 minutes

Materials: cardboard, pencils, rulers, tape, scissors, paint, paintbrushes

When people think of Egypt, they often think of the majestic pyramids. Students can try their hand at assembling and decorating their own pyramids. The pattern for a pyramid is simple. Using the rulers and pencils, have students draw four triangles of equal size on the cardboard and then cut them out. They should tape the sides together from the inside, so that the paint will adhere better to the outside of the pyramid. Once the pyramids are assembled, students should use paint to decorate them. Challenge students to choose an ancient Egyptian symbol to paint on the sides. As students finish painting, have them explain the importance of pyramids in ancient Egypt.

Fertile Crescent Rest Stop   👤 individual   🕐 20 minutes

Materials: unlined paper, colored pencils or markers

Traders often traveled in caravans for safety. They made long treks on donkeys across the Fertile Crescent to trade goods. Travel was difficult and dangerous at times. Ask your students to imagine they are the owners of a rest stop in the Fertile Crescent. Students should design colorful flyers or brochures to lure tired traders to their rest stops. Encourage your students to think about the traveling conditions of the traders and then design their ads based on what would matter most to a weary traveler. Students should be as creative as possible in designing their ads. Display the ads in the classroom when students are finished.

Making Cuneiform Tablets

👫 partners   🕐 30 minutes

Materials: clay, craft sticks (or other instrument for writing on clay), resource materials

Before paper was invented, ancient scribes wrote on clay tablets. They used wedge-shaped symbols called cuneiform. Give each pair of students enough clay to make small tablets. Students must flatten, shape, and smooth the clay so they can write on it with their writing instruments. Students may use resource materials to find examples of cuneiform. They should then take turns making the actual symbols on the clay tablets with their writing instruments. Ask students to share how their writing would be different if they still had to write on clay instead of using paper or a computer.

Systems of Writing

👥 small group   🕐 30 minutes

Materials: resource materials

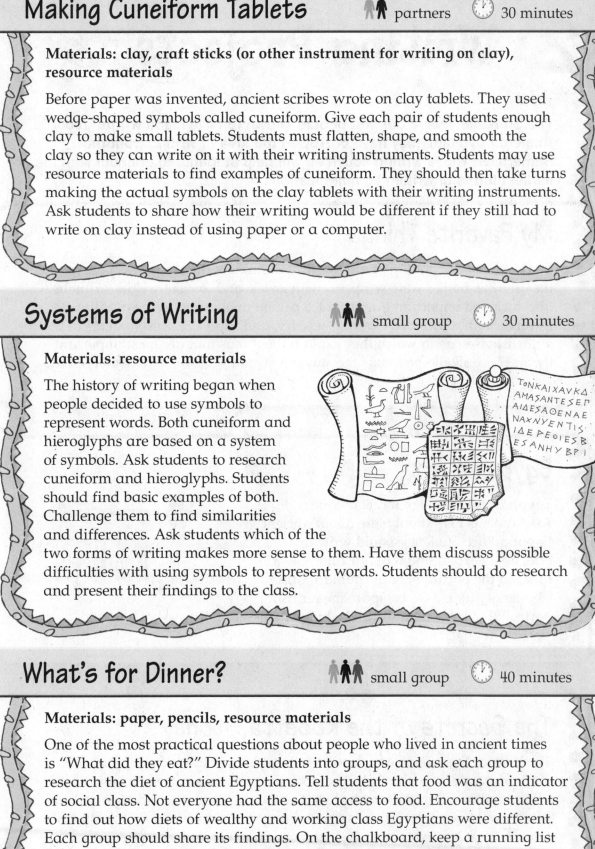

The history of writing began when people decided to use symbols to represent words. Both cuneiform and hieroglyphs are based on a system of symbols. Ask students to research cuneiform and hieroglyphs. Students should find basic examples of both. Challenge them to find similarities and differences. Ask students which of the two forms of writing makes more sense to them. Have them discuss possible difficulties with using symbols to represent words. Students should do research and present their findings to the class.

What's for Dinner?

👥 small group   🕐 40 minutes

Materials: paper, pencils, resource materials

One of the most practical questions about people who lived in ancient times is "What did they eat?" Divide students into groups, and ask each group to research the diet of ancient Egyptians. Tell students that food was an indicator of social class. Not everyone had the same access to food. Encourage students to find out how diets of wealthy and working class Egyptians were different. Each group should share its findings. On the chalkboard, keep a running list of new information about the diets of ancient Egyptians.

© Harcourt

2 Writing Projects

The Sumerians were the first people known to have made written records. Ancient Egyptians may have borrowed the idea of writing from the Sumerians. These writing activities will help students to connect with the earliest forms of written communication.

My Favorite Things

The tombs of ancient Egyptians show how strongly the Egyptians believed in the afterlife. Bodies were wrapped with jewels and ancient writings. Tombs also included important things that a person might need in the afterlife. For example, tombs included clothing, jewelry, and furniture. Ask students to write a narrative essay in which they explain the things that are most important to them. These should be things the students would want to be remembered by.

Egyptian Art

Egyptian art is known for its unique style. Ask students to find out more about ancient Egyptian art. Students should write a brief essay explaining the style and how it affected the portrayal of the human form. Challenge students to compare the realistic portrayal of some animals to the highly artificial portrayal of humans.

The Secrets of the Rosetta Stone

The Rosetta Stone enabled scientists to interpret ancient hieroglyphics. It is a vital primary source that helped unlock the mysteries of the symbolic writings. What kind of writings do we have today that explain our language and culture? What would give the best clues about what our lives were like? Ask students to write an essay explaining their choices. Students may choose American or international writing samples. They could choose dictionaries, government documents, and so on.

Write Your Own Hieroglyphs

Review the Egyptian hieroglyphs on page 144 of the Student Edition and the English meanings for each symbol. Challenge students to write their own system of hieroglyphs. Students should choose 10 to 15 high-frequency words and design symbols to stand for each word. Students should then write a sentence or two using their own symbols.

Letter of Protest

Around 2000 B.C. Egypt attempted to annex Nubia in order to control the trade routes that the Nubians had established. Have students review the information in their textbooks about the annexation of Nubia (or have them do additional research on their own), and then ask each student to write a letter of protest about the annexation. Ask students to imagine that they are Nubian citizens who strongly oppose Egypt's plans for control of the land. Students should give reasons why the annexation is unfair.

River Valley Poem

The earliest communities lived in river valleys. Rivers gave people water for cooking, bathing, and drinking. Fishermen fed their families from the life-giving waters. Ask students to honor the rivers and the river valleys in a poem. Students should imagine that they are inhabitants of this fertile area and that they are grateful for the life the river provides for them. Challenge students to use sensory details.

Daily Geography

1. **Human-Environment Interactions**   Why did early people settle near river valleys?

2. **Regions**   What were the three major river valleys in which the first known civilizations developed?

3. **Human-Environment Interactions**   What did early people learn to dig to control river flooding and irrigate crops?

4. **Regions**   In which region would you find Sumer?

5. **Place**   What is the name of "the land between the rivers"?

6. **Place**   On which kind of landform is northern Mesopotamia located?

7. **Place**   What are the smaller rivers that flow into the Tigris called?

8. **Human-Environment Interactions**   What is the name of the first known settlement in southern Mesopotamia?

9. **Location**   Which four Sumerian cities developed into the world's first city-states?

10. **Movement**   What were groups of traders traveling together by donkey called?

11. **Location**   The city of Ur once lay close to a river that has changed course many times. What is this river called?

12. **Human-Environment Interactions**   What most likely destroyed the city of Ur soon after it was built?

13. **Human-Environment Interactions**   What was the name of the tallest building in every city-state?

14. **Human-Environment Interactions**   Which group of people first attached wheels to carts?

© Harcourt

15. **Location**   In which city in central Mesopotamia did the conqueror Sargon set up his capital?

16. **Movement**   In which direction does the Nile River flow?

17. **Regions**   Which three regions can be found along the Nile River?

18. **Place**   Which of the following is a triangle-shaped piece of land formed at the mouth of some rivers?
delta   plateau
cataract   inlet

19. **Movement**   Traders in Egypt were connected with traders in southwestern Asia by which landform?

20. **Location**   What was the name of the new capital of the united lands of Upper and Lower Egypt?

21. **Human-Environment Interactions**   What is the name of the best-known Egyptian pyramid?

22. **Movement**   What group of people crossed from southwestern Asia into Egypt by way of the Sinai Peninsula?

23. **Regions**   In which area did the Kush civilization begin?

24. **Location**   What was the main source of water for ancient Nubians?

25. **Location**   What do modern historians call the ancient kingdom of Kush?

26. **Location**   By 800 B.C. the Kushites had built a new capital city farther south on the Nile. What was the name of the capital?

27. **Location**   Around 591 B.C. Kushite leaders moved the capital again. What was its new location?

28. **Human-Environment Interactions**   When did the period of Kush achievement known as the Meroitic period begin? When did it end?

29. **Human-Environment Interactions**   What caused the people in the city of Meroë to become very wealthy?

30. **Human-Environment Interactions**   How did Greek rulers affect the success of trade in Meroë?

© Harcourt

Why Character Counts

- Respect
- **Fairness**
- Responsibility
- Patriotism
- Caring
- Trustworthiness

Fairness

What do you think of when you hear the word *fairness*? Fairness means treating someone with honesty and without prejudice. Fairness can mean different things to different people. What seems fair, or right, to one person may not seem fair to another person. That is the reason that we have laws that govern many areas of our lives. The idea is that all people should be treated equally under the law.

Hammurabi was an emperor who was very concerned with fairness. He is probably most famous for the list of 282 laws that he compiled. These laws are known as the Code of Hammurabi. When Hammurabi became emperor of the Babylonian Empire, he gathered all the laws from the city-states he had conquered and rewrote them into one set of laws. Hammurabi hoped to make the laws fairer and to keep the more powerful people in society from taking advantage of the weaker people.

Today, fairness is important in business deals. People use contracts, or written agreements, to protect them in a court of law. Another area where fairness is considered critical is in sports. Referees and umpires function as judges on the field of play. Fairness is important in every aspect of our lives from our families to the highest courts of law.

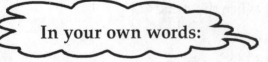

In your own words:

Write a definition for the word *fairness*.

_____

_____

Name _____

Character Activity

Imagine that you are a middle-school principal and that you have two students in your office who have been accused of fighting on school property. The rules of the school clearly forbid fighting, but one student claims that the other made fun of his little sister. Your job is to treat each of the students fairly. How will you handle the situation? Write about how you will deal with each of the students fairly. Make sure you give reasons for your decisions.

_____

_____

_____

_____

_____

_____

_____

_____

_____

_____

_____

_____

_____

_____

_____

_____

Economic Literacy

Cost-Benefit Analysis

Have you ever wanted to buy something that was really expensive? Have you wondered if it would be worth the cost? If so, you have done a cost-benefit analysis. A cost-benefit analysis is weighing the cost of an item against the benefit of owning the item.

Traders in ancient times had to make cost-benefit analyses all the time. Egyptians carried on trade with parts of Asia, Africa, and other areas in the Mediterranean region. Anyone who was able to safely carry goods from one area to another could make a lot of money. But trade was risky. On land, caravans moved very slowly. Traders in caravans had to worry about being robbed while on their journeys. Trade by sea was quicker, but pirates were a threat. If traders were robbed, they lost everything. Bad weather was also a problem on land or sea.

Many people do cost-benefit analyses on a regular basis. People must decide if an item is worth a certain price at a certain time. Ask yourself if you have to have the item now or if you can wait a little bit. And try to avoid impulse buying. That's buying something on the spot just because you want it. If you decide to buy something immediately, you may not have enough time to do a cost-benefit analysis and determine whether it's really worth it.

Name _____

Cost-Benefit Analysis Activity

 Think of a time when you did a cost-benefit analysis. What were you planning to buy? Did you decide that it was worth it to purchase the item at the time, or did you decide to wait? Explain your reasoning.

_____

_____

_____

_____

_____

Think of something that you would like to buy now. Do a cost-benefit analysis of the item and explain your thinking. What benefits would there be to getting the item now, and what benefits would there be if you waited? What factors influenced your decision?

_____

_____

_____

_____

_____

_____

_____

_____

_____

Citizenship

> **Read About It**   Have you ever heard the word *legislature*? A legislature is an organized group that has the authority to make and change laws. In the United States, there are three branches of government—the executive branch, the judicial branch, and the legislative branch. The legislative branch of government is made up of the Senate and the House of Representatives. These two bodies are responsible for making the laws for citizens of the United States. In Sumer, the city-states started out being governed by a group of leaders, but then moved to being ruled by only one leader, a priest-king or en. Sumerians formed the world's first monarchy, a governing system ruled by a king or queen. Very few countries are ruled by monarchies today.

1. Do you think having three branches of government might be better than having only one branch? Why or why not?

   _____

   _____

   _____

   _____

2. What kinds of problems might arise in a monarchy?

   _____

   _____

   _____

   _____

> **Talk About It**   How were the monarchs in Sumerian times usually chosen? How is this method different than the way we choose most leaders in the United States? Which type of government do you think is more effective and why?

© Harcourt

Name _____

Write About It The United States government uses a system called checks and balances to make sure no one branch of government becomes too powerful. A law must be tested in all branches of government. If the president disagrees with a law proposed by the legislative branch, he may veto, or reject, the law. The judicial branch tests laws in the court system. If a law does not hold up, it may need to be changed. Is this system of government fair? Write about why people might disagree about laws and why you think some laws are rewritten.

_____

_____

_____

_____

_____

_____

_____

_____

_____

_____

_____

_____

_____

Create a Postage Stamp
Unit 3

Materials needed:
*Sheets of drawing paper

*Colored pencils

*Construction paper

*Scissors

*Glue

*Fine-tip markers

Social Studies Skills:
*Using Visuals

*Israel

*Judah

Reading Skills:
*Cause and Effect

*Point of View

*Categorize

Instructions:
1. On the top half of a sheet of drawing paper, design a postage stamp similar to the example shown. Then plan a stamp that represents either Israel or Judah.

2. Draw your design in the large stamp on the drawing paper. Outline it in marker, and color it in with colored pencils.

Illustrations:

© Harcourt

3. Below the stamp explain what your stamp represents and why you chose the subject of your design.

4. Glue the completed stamp sheet to a sheet of construction paper.

5. The teacher may wish to display completed stamps in the classroom.

My stamp is of the Ten Commandments

My stamp represents Israel. I chose the Ten Commandments because they were such an important part of the lives of the Israelites. According to the Bible, God gave Moses the Ten Commandments on Mount Sinai. The commandments were a collection of laws that became part of Judaism.

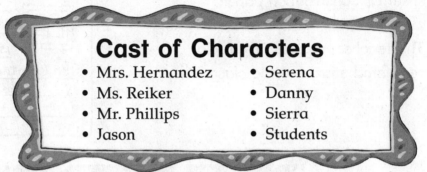

**Drama
ACTIVITY**

ANCIENT HEBREWS HALL OF FAME

In this drama, you will hear about the people who shaped ancient Hebrew history. A pair of guest speakers has come to a sixth-grade social studies class to introduce students to some of the most significant characters in ancient Hebrew history.

Cast of Characters
- Mrs. Hernandez
- Ms. Reiker
- Mr. Phillips
- Jason
- Serena
- Danny
- Sierra
- Students

MRS. HERNANDEZ: (*standing in front of the class*) Class, could I have your attention please? I'd like to introduce you to our two guest speakers today. Ms. Reiker and Mr. Phillips are both students at Key College. They are studying the Ancient Hebrews, and they have kindly agreed to come in today to introduce our unit.

MR. PHILLIPS: Hi everyone. What we'd like to do today is give you an overview of some important people. This way when you come across these characters while you're studying, you'll already know a little about them.

MS. REIKER: If any of you has a question while we're speaking, please don't hesitate to ask.

MR. PHILLIPS: Alright, let's get started. How many of you have ever heard of Abraham?

JASON: (*raising his hand*) I have.

MR. PHILLIPS: Great. What do you know about him?

JASON: He's the guy who got the Ten Commandments, right?

MS. REIKER: Well, not quite. Abraham is known as the father of the Ancient Hebrews. He was born about 2000 B.C. Stories in the Bible say that God spoke to Abraham and told him to move to Canaan. So Abraham listened.

© Harcourt

Social Studies

SERENA:	(*raising her hand*) You mean he just picked up and left his home? Just like that?
MR. PHILLIPS:	Not only did he leave his home, he took his whole family with him. He had to cross the desert to reach Canaan. Here's where he started in Mesopotamia (*holds up a map and points to Mesopotamia*). He had to go here (*points to Canaan*).
MS. REIKER:	And once Abraham got to Canaan, the Bible says that Abraham and God made a covenant together.
SIERRA:	What is a covenant?
MR. PHILLIPS:	A covenant is a special agreement. In this covenant, God promised Abraham that Canaan would always belong to his family and his descendents. And in return, Abraham promised to only worship God. The name Abraham actually means "father of many."
MS. REIKER:	Abraham's great grandson was very important too. His name was Joseph. Now, let me ask you this question—have you ever been really, really angry with a little brother or sister? (*class nods and says "yes"*)
DANNY:	I get so angry with my little brother that sometimes I want to give him away.
MR. PHILLIPS:	That's funny you should say that because Joseph's brothers did basically the same thing.
STUDENTS:	(*together*) What?

MR. PHILLIPS:	Here's what happened. Joseph's father was named Jacob. Jacob had twelve sons in all, but he liked Joseph the best. So, he gave Joseph this fantastic present—a beautiful coat of many colors.
SIERRA:	I'll bet his brothers were furious!
MS. REIKER:	They were completely furious. They actually sold Joseph to traveling traders who were headed for Egypt. Then they went home and told their father, Jacob, that a wild animal had killed Joseph.
MR. PHILLIPS:	And here's where the story gets really interesting. Joseph did go to Egypt, but he was so smart that he attracted the attention of the Egyptian pharaoh. Over time, Joseph got to be second in command in Egypt.
DANNY:	So everything turned out OK for him, right?
MR. PHILLIPS:	Things were looking OK for Joseph, but not for his family back home. Back in Canaan there was a famine. Does anyone know what a famine is?
SERENA:	I do. It means there wasn't enough food to eat.
MR. PHILLIPS:	Exactly. But remember that Joseph's family still lived in Canaan. So Jacob sent his sons to Egypt to buy food. Guess who they had to buy food from?
MS. REIKER:	Can you imagine going to Egypt and finding the brother you had sold into slavery as second in command? The brothers were completely terrified when they found out. They were sure that Joseph would take revenge on them.
DANNY:	So what happened? Did Joseph get back at his brothers? I sure would have.
MS. REIKER:	Amazingly, Joseph decided to forgive his brothers, and eventually, the rest of the family moved to Egypt. And Jacob's sons became leaders of different tribes.
MR. PHILLIPS:	Now, let's move on to another very famous person—Moses.
JASON:	OK, so that's the guy that got the Ten Commandments, right?
MR. PHILLIPS:	That's right. What do you know about the Ten Commandments?

SIERRA:	Oh, I know. They tell you what not to do.
MS. REIKER:	(*chuckling*) Well, it's a little more complicated than that, but basically you're correct. The Ten Commandments became a very important part of the law. People lived according to them.
MRS. HERNANDEZ:	(*addressing Mr. Phillips and Ms. Reiker*) I hate to interrupt, but I think we have time to hear about one more person.
MS. REIKER:	(*looking at her watch*) Oh no, there are so many other people to discuss. Well, Mr. Phillips, whom should we pick?
MR. PHILLIPS:	I think we should close by telling the students about King Solomon. He probably made the biggest changes of all the early ancient Hebrew kings.
MS. REIKER:	Sounds good. Well, as Mr. Phillips said, Solomon was a very important king to the ancient Hebrews. He was the son of David, who had been king before him. Solomon had big plans. He wanted to build a temple in Jerusalem.
MR. PHILLIPS:	That's right. He wanted to build the temple for a special purpose. Not only did Solomon want a place for the ancient Hebrews to worship, but he also wanted a very special place to keep the Ark of the Covenant. Does anyone know what was stored in the Ark of the Covenant?
JASON:	I thought the ark was the thing all the animals got on. You know, Noah and the ark?
MS. REIKER:	(*smiling*) Well, that's a different kind of ark entirely. The Ark of the Covenant is the box where the Ten Commandments were kept. The box was very, very special and sacred to the ancient Hebrews. So Solomon built a temple. But he also built many other things.
MRS. HERNANDEZ:	(*standing up from her place at her desk*) Well, unfortunately, that's all we have time for today. Thank you both so much. I think the students have a better idea about some of the key people they'll be reading about and studying.
MS. REIKER:	Thanks for having us, everyone. We enjoyed it.
MR. PHILLIPS:	Thanks, boys and girls. We'll see you later (*waving and heading for the door of the classroom*).
STUDENTS:	Thanks for coming (*students applaud*).

THE END

Simulations and Games

TIC-TAC-TOE WITH A TWIST This is a twist on an old classic. Divide the class into two teams. Ask each team to devise a list of ten to fifteen questions, depending on the time allotted. The questions should be based on material found in the unit. The questions should start simply and get increasingly difficult. Quickly review each team's questions to ensure fair play, and then draw a giant tic-tac-toe grid on the board. Flip a coin to determine which team goes first. Each team should appoint one person to read the questions as needed. A team must answer a question correctly to be able to put an *X* or *O* on the board. No student may answer a question twice. This should encourage as many students to participate as possible. Play until a team wins. *GAME*

Who am I?

Moses?

Solomon?

Cyrus?

WHO AM I? Make a list of the people related to the unit. Divide the class into two groups. Randomly assign half the names to each group. Ask each group to write two clues for each character. The first clue should be more difficult than the second clue. Make sure that all students are participating in writing the clues. When students have finished writing the clues, begin the game. Teams should go back and forth reading clues and trying to guess which character from the unit is being described. If a team can guess the character with only one clue, the answer is worth two points. If the second clue must be given, the correct answer is worth only one point. If a team guesses incorrectly, no points are awarded. Play until all characters have been described. The team with the most points wins. *GAME*

FILL IN THE BLANKS

This game will test the students' knowledge of the vocabulary, people, and places in the unit. Divide the class into two teams, A and B. Use the vocabulary, people, and places lists provided on the first pages of each lesson as the word bank. On the chalkboard, draw letter blanks to represent one of the words from the word bank. Ask Team A to guess letters to fill in the blanks. When Team A guesses an incorrect letter, play switches to Team B. The first team to guess the word correctly gets a point; however, a team may only guess the word if it is their turn to play. If the word is guessed incorrectly, play automatically moves to the other team. For variety you could allow students to guess consonants only and not vowels. After each word is correctly guessed, draw new letter blanks on the board to represent a new word. Play continues until one team has earned a specified number of points or until time runs out. *GAME*

HELP! I'M STRANDED!

This game will help test the students' understanding of the places mentioned in the unit. Divide students into groups of about five or six students. Ask each group member to choose a place mentioned in the unit. Students should not tell other group members the place they have selected. Tell students that they should pretend that they are stranded in their chosen place and only their group members can rescue them. Group members can rescue their teammate by correctly guessing his or her location. One group member should be chosen to be the first stranded person. The stranded group member should give a detailed description to other group members explaining where he or she is. After the description has been given, the group members must try to figure out the location. The person who correctly guesses where the group member was located will earn a point. Play rotates until all group members have had a chance to be stranded. The person with the most points at the end wins. *GAME*

© Harcourt

UNIT 3 Long-Term Project

HEBREW PEOPLE—A STORY IN PICTURES

In this project, students will collect images and information that represent the long history of the Hebrew people. The final product will be a collection of montages that can be displayed on a bulletin board in the classroom.

Materials: paper, pencils, resource materials

 Week 1   👥👤 group   🕐 30 minutes

Introduce the topic by having students close their eyes and think about different periods in their lives—early childhood, elementary school, middle school. Ask them to think of images that capture the essence of each of those periods in time. In much the same way, students will create a montage—a collection of images—to illustrate the history of the Hebrew people.

Break students into five groups, and assign each group one of the following topics: Abraham, Joseph, and slavery in Egypt; Moses and the Exodus; The Kings of Israel—Saul, David, and Solomon; A House Divided—Israel and Judah; Conquerors—Assyria, Babylon, Persia, and Macedonia. Encourage the groups to think up a list of images or artifacts that capture their topic and have them record their thoughts. Outside of class, students should gather a variety of images. In some cases, students may want to draw, paint, or sketch original images. Tell students that as they research images, they should also start to think about the story they will present along with their final montage. For next week, ask students to bring in all of the images they find.

Week 2   👤👥👤 group   🕐 45 minutes

Materials: paper, pencils, resource materials

This week students should focus on sorting through the images they have brought with them to class. Students should begin to plan their montages, but will probably need additional time to continue researching pictures and other items. The rest of the time should be spent finding whatever additional resources are necessary to complete their montages. Students should also decide whether they will need to draw any pictures for their montages.

© Harcourt

Week 3

 group   🕐 45 minutes

Materials: images, posterboard, scissors, glue, markers

Students should work on creating their montages this week. Have groups decide on the final number of pictures that they will use and encourage them to lay out the posterboard and carefully plan the space they have to use. If students have included drawings, they should be completed this week as well. As students assemble their montages, have them develop the story they wish to tell with their pictures. Tell students that next week they will display their montages on the bulletin board and talk about them.

HISTORY OF THE HEBREW PEOPLE

Week 4

👪 group   🕐 45 minutes

Materials: completed montages

This week students should put any necessary finishing touches on their montages and then take turns presenting them to the class. Students should explain why they chose the images they did and highlight any with special significance. Groups should present in order starting with Abraham, Joseph, and slavery in Egypt. As groups finish, display their artwork on the bulletin board. When all groups have finished, encourage the class to view the bulletin board as one complete montage.

Tips for combination classrooms:

5-6 For grade five, add information about American Indians and their encounters with the settlers.

6-7 For grade seven, you may want to discuss China in the Middle Ages. Topics could include the Tang dynasty, Buddhism, the Sung period, the Mongol period, and the Ming dynasty.

UNIT 3 Short-Term Projects

The history of Israel is rich with symbols. From the Temple to the Ten Commandments to the Seder, students can experience a part of Israel's past and present.

Temple Layout
👤 individual ⏰ 30 minutes

Materials: unlined paper, colored pencils or markers, resource materials

King Solomon set out to build a temple in Jerusalem. He wanted the people of Israel to have a place to worship. He also wanted to keep the Ark of the Covenant in a safe and sacred place. Have students research the design and layout of Solomon's temple. Students should pay particular attention to how the inside of the temple was designed. Ask students to draw and label diagrams of King Solomon's temple.

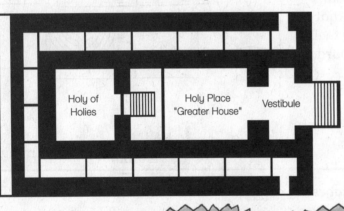

Messages in Hebrew
👥 partners ⏰ 30 minutes

Materials: paper, pens, pencils, resource materials

Most of the literary works from ancient Israel were written using the Hebrew alphabet. The Hebrew alphabet is made up of letters that represent certain sounds, like the English alphabet. Invite students to perform research to find a table that shows what letters in the Hebrew alphabet are equivalent to English letters. This table could also be provided for the students. Divide students into pairs. Challenge students to use the Hebrew alphabet to write a message to their partner. The message that students write should describe a fact that students have learned in the unit. Remind students that Hebrew writing goes from right to left. After the messages have been written, students should exchange their messages with their partner and try to decipher the message.

© Harcourt

The Passover Seder

Materials: resource materials, markers, posterboard

Every spring Jewish people celebrate Passover to remember their escape from slavery in Egypt to freedom in the promised land. Break students into small groups and ask them to research the following questions about the Passover Seder: What are the special elements of the Seder? What does each of these elements represent? What is the *Afikomen*, and what happens to it? How are children a special part of the Seder? When each group has completed its research, students should design a small poster that shows the major elements of the Passover Seder. Display each group's poster in the classroom.

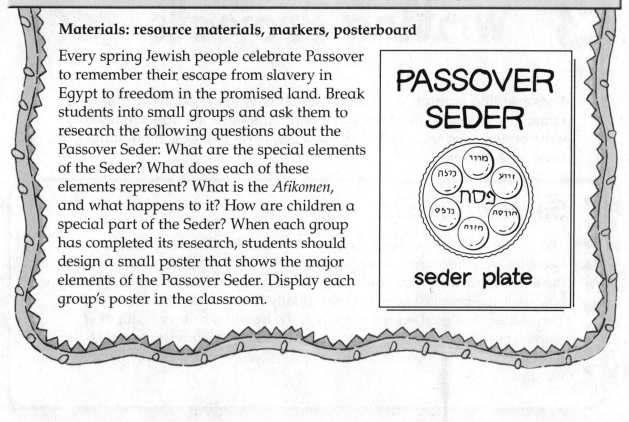

Compare Maps

Materials: resource materials, pencils, paper

The land of the kingdom of Israel has been in a state of change since ancient times. The land was quite extensive under Kings David and Solomon, but today, Israel occupies a much smaller geographical area. Break students into small groups and have them research maps of ancient Israel and compare them with modern-day maps of the regions. Have them write down the differences they see. If time allows, ask students to further research Israel's changing boundaries between ancient times and today. Encourage them to find additional maps that show boundary lines.

Writing Projects

These writing prompts encourage students to experience the history of Israel in a variety of different ways. Students have the opportunity to write songs, proverbs, textbook sections, royal decrees, biographies, and newspaper articles.

Songs of Exodus

The people of Israel were enslaved by the pharaoh of Egypt. Eventually, the Israelites were freed from slavery. The Israelites left Egypt in a huge mass called the Exodus. In pairs, have students write songs of Exodus. Ask them to imagine how the Israelites must have felt after finally being freed from the Egyptians. Their songs should reflect the feelings of the Israelites as they begin their journey out of Egypt. If they wish, students may set their lyrics to a tune that most people know. Students can share their songs with the class when they are finished.

Solomon's Proverbs

Solomon is credited with writing the Book of Proverbs in the Bible. Proverbs are short sayings that express important truths. Have students review proverbs from the unit to gain an understanding of the type of message a proverb communicates. Then ask students to practice writing three to five proverbs on their own. The proverbs should express universal truths and should be broad enough to apply to a wide range of people.

Geography and Conflict

The geography of a region can sometimes contribute to the way of life there. Many conflicts arose in the ancient kingdom of Israel. How might the geography of the region have contributed to the conflict of the region? Invite students to research the geography of the kingdom of Israel. Tell them to imagine that a textbook is being created about ancient Israel, and they have been hired to write a brief section discussing how geography led to conflict. Remind students that their audience would be students so they should write with students in mind.

© Harcourt

Cyrus's Plan

When Cyrus, ruler of the Persian Empire, conquered Babylon, he decreed that as long as the people accepted his rule, he would accept their current religious beliefs. He allowed the Israelites back into Judah and to rebuild the Temple. Have students imagine that they are each in the role of Cyrus. Challenge them to write a decree that explains why they will allow the Israelites to practice their religion, as opposed to trying to force them to change it as other rulers have done.

A King's Biography

Before the kingdom of Israel split into two distinct parts, three kings ruled the land—Saul, David, and Solomon. It was when Solomon's son Rehoboam became king that the kingdom of Israel was divided. Encourage students to research the life of one of the three kings and write a biography about him. Students should look beyond the information contained in the textbook. Ask students to find information about the king's accomplishments, as well as information about his family in an attempt to present a well-rounded view of the king in the biography.

Biography of a King

Chronicling the Split

The kingdom of Israel split into two parts—Israel and Judah—after a rebellion of the northern tribes. The tribes did not agree with the plans Rehoboam had for Israel, and the tribes also thought that Rehoboam had shown favoritism to his own tribe of Judah. Have students write an imaginary newspaper article for the day after the northern tribes rebelled. The article should be factually based and should attempt to answer the questions Who, What, Where, When, Why, and How. Students may need to do some additional research before writing the article. As an added twist, you may instruct students to write the article from one of two points of view—either that of a northern tribe or a tribe still loyal to Rehoboam.

1. **Place**   Where was Abraham born?

2. **Movement**   According to the Bible, Abraham traveled with his family across the
                      desert to which land?

3. **Location**   The land of Canaan borders which body of water?

4. **Movement**   In which direction would an ancient trader travel to get from Canaan
                      to Egypt?

5. **Location**   On which continent is Egypt located?

6. **Place**   According to the Bible, where did the Egyptian pharaoh order that all
                      Israelite baby boys be drowned?

7. **Movement**   What is the Israelites' freedom from slavery called?

8. **Movement**   After the Israelites left Egypt, they traveled on which peninsula along
                      the Red Sea?

9. **Location**   Forty years after leaving Egypt, where did the Israelites settle?

10. **Location**   Was the land of Phoenicia located north or south of the land of Israel?

11. **Regions**   Under King David's rule, the kingdom of Israel eventually stretched
                      between which two regions?

12. **Place**   Which city did King David name as the new capital of Israel?

13. **Place**   The ancient land of Philistia bordered which body of water?

14. **Location**   With which two neighboring lands did Israel form trade agreements
                      under King Solomon?

15. **Regions**   What portion of the kingdom of Israel disliked Solomon and believed
                      that he showed favoritism to his own tribe?

© Harcourt

16. **Regions** What were the names of the two parts of the kingdom of Israel after it split?

17. **Place** What were the names of the capital cities of Israel and Judah?

18. **Regions** From which part of the world did the Assyrians come?

19. **Place** Sargon II said, "I led away 27,290 of its inhabitants as captives. . . . I have rebuilt the city better than it had been before and settled it with people which I brought from the lands of my conquests." Of which city was Sargon II speaking?

20. **Location** Which river lay east of Samaria?

21. **Place** In 597 B.C., the Babylonians conquered which land?

22. **Movement** What happened during the Babylonian Captivity?

23. **Human-Environment Interactions** In 538 B.C., who conquered Babylon?

24. **Human-Environment Interactions** What did King Cyrus allow the Israelites to do?

25. **Movement** What was the scattering of Jews outside their homeland called?

26. **Location** In 332 B.C., the Judaeans were conquered by the emperor Alexander the Great. Where was Alexander from?

27. **Human-Environment Interactions** What holy sites were completely destroyed by the Romans in A.D. 70?

28. **Place** Where did Rabbi Yohanan ben Zaccai found a Jewish school to help preserve Jewish life and culture?

29. **Movement** Who sent Judaeans into exile in A.D. 132?

30. **Human-Environment Interactions** Which two world religions did Judaism influence?

Why Character Counts

- Respect
- Fairness
- **Responsibility**
- Patriotism
- Caring
- Trustworthiness

Responsibility

Responsibility means being accountable for your actions. That means you don't blame someone else for something you did. Responsibility also means that you show trustworthiness and dependability when you are given a job to do.

Israelite kings, such as David and Solomon, showed responsibility in their jobs as leaders of Israel. They worked hard to protect the people of Israel. As rulers, they took their jobs seriously. The Israelites knew they could depend on David and Solomon to govern wisely. Today, we expect our leaders to act responsibly as well. The most important thing, however, is to take personal responsibility for our own lives and actions. We must act responsibly even when others don't.

In your own words:

Write a definition for the word *responsibility*.

_____

_____

_____

© Harcourt

Character Activity

Imagine that your sixth-grade class has been asked to write a short skit about responsibility and perform the skit at a school assembly. Your skit should clearly show what responsibility is and how young people can act responsibly when faced with a difficult situation. On the lines below, write a skit about responsibility that other students would understand and enjoy.

_____

_____

_____

_____

_____

_____

_____

_____

_____

_____

_____

_____

_____

_____

_____

_____

3 Economic Literacy

Taxes

Have you ever been paid money for doing chores around the house? If your parents paid you, you probably got to keep all the money. When adults are paid for their jobs, however, they must give a portion of that money back to the government in taxes. Tax is money charged by the government to citizens. The money is used for public purposes, such as roads, schools, and law enforcement.

King Solomon was known not only for his wisdom but also for his building projects. He was responsible for building a temple in Jerusalem, as well as forts, grain storehouses, and water systems. To help pay for these projects, Solomon taxed the people of Israel. Although the kingdom of Israel grew under King Solomon's reign, some people thought that the taxes were too high. They did not like having to pay so much to the king for his projects.

There are many different kinds of taxes in the United States today. There is sales tax, a tax you pay on things that you buy, and there is income tax, a tax you pay based on how much money you make. And there is also property tax if you own your home. Some of these taxes go to the state and federal governments for a huge variety of programs that are intended to benefit everyone. Some people don't like paying taxes but they know that it is necessary to support the government.

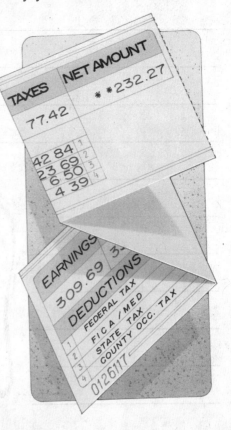

© Harcourt

Name _____

Tax Activity

Some people think taxes are fair, and some don't, depending on how the tax money is used. On the lines below, write about how you would like to see government put tax money to use. Then write about a way government could use tax money that you would call unfair.

_____

_____

_____

_____

_____

_____

What do you think about the taxes you will have to pay as you get older? Do you think it is fair to charge sales tax, for example? Write your impressions of the American tax system on the lines below. If you have more questions about taxes, write them below as well and then ask your parents or teachers for the answers.

_____

_____

_____

_____

_____

_____

_____

UNIT

3 Citizenship

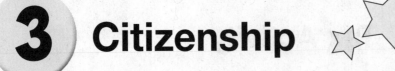

> **Read About It**   The Bill of Rights, which was adopted on December 15, 1791, contains ten amendments to the Constitution. The First Amendment guarantees freedom of religion. It also guarantees freedom of speech and of the press. The first part of the amendment reads, "Congress shall make no law respecting an establishment of religion, or prohibiting the free exercise thereof . . ." That means that people are free to have and express religious beliefs without any interference from the government. It also means that if people do not wish to hold to any particular religious ideas, they do not have to. In ancient times, Cyrus, leader of the Persian Empire, decided to allow Israelites to practice their own religion as long as they obeyed the rules of the new government. In this way, Cyrus was allowing freedom of religion to his people.

What does freedom of religion mean to you?

_____

_____

_____

How can you tell that people in the United States have freedom of religion? Write at least two examples of freedom of religion in this country.

_____

_____

_____

_____

_____

_____

© Harcourt

Name _____

● ▸ **Talk About It** What are some of the reasons that freedom of religion can still be a touchy topic in the United States? Weren't all problems addressed by the passage of the First Amendment? What changes, if any, do you think should be made in our culture with regard to freedom of religion?

▸ **Write About It** Why was freedom of religion important to the early Jewish people? Were there times when the Jews were not allowed to freely express their religious beliefs? How did it affect the Jews when their beliefs were not tolerated? Write an essay in which you answer these questions. Make sure to support your essay with examples.

_____

_____

_____

_____

_____

_____

_____

_____

_____

_____

_____

_____

_____

Plate Book
Unit 4

Materials needed:
*3 white paper plates

*Markers, crayons, or colored
 pencils

*Scissors

*Glue

Social Studies Skills:
*Comparing Places

*Cultures

*Opportunities

Reading Skills:
*Summarize

*Draw Conclusions

*Point of View

Instructions:

1. Fold the first paper plate in half.
   Cut out a narrow window along
   the fold between the ruffled
   edges.

2. Fold the second paper plate in
   half. Cut a slit from the edge of
   the plate to the inner edge of
   the ruffle (about 1" long). Make a
   second slit directly opposite the
   first.

Illustrations:

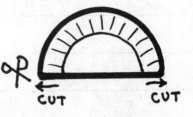

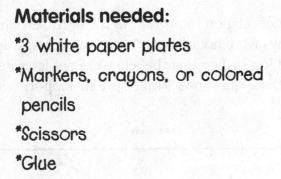

© Harcourt

3. Open the second paper plate. Fold it in half the other way without creasing it so that the two slits meet. Push the folded second plate halfway through the window of the first plate. Open the plate, sliding one slit past each end of the window to lock the plates together.

4. Repeat steps 2 and 3 with the third plate.

5. Close the booklet and title it "Athens and Sparta." Use the first three pages to illustrate and compare the geographic regions, governments, and cultures of the two city-states. You can make a word web to explain your ideas.

6. On the last two pages, fill in the vocabulary words and important facts from the unit.

7. Draw conclusions about the two city-states as you compare them.

© Harcourt

ANTIGONE—AN ADAPTATION

Antigone is the third play in the Oedipus trilogy written by Sophocles. It is a tragic story of a young woman who does what she believes is right in spite of the fact that she must break the law to do so. Antigone has one sister, Ismene, and two brothers, Eteocles and Polyneices. Her father, Oedipus, has been killed, and her brothers are ready to fight for the throne of Thebes. Eteocles fights in support of his Uncle Creon, Oedipus's brother, but Polyneices fights against his brother and uncle. The brothers kill each other in battle, but because Polyneices fought against his own city, Uncle Creon, the new king of Thebes, declares him to be a traitor and refuses to allow him to be buried. Antigone is beside herself with grief and thinks that no matter what her brother has done, he deserves to be buried. She takes it upon herself to bury him, and her uncle condemns her to death for breaking his law.

You have just read about a portion of the play *Antigone*. More of the play follows. It has been put into more modern language to make it easier to read.

Cast of Characters

- Antigone
- Ismene
- Chorus Member 1
- Chorus Member 2
- Creon
- Guard

[*It is dawn, and Antigone and Ismene are talking outside the palace gates. They are discussing their uncle's decree regarding Polyneices.*]

© Harcourt

ACT I

ANTIGONE: Ismene, my dear sister, is there anything else that can happen to us now? Will Zeus bring even more sadness and shame on our household? Have you heard about the new decree from our Uncle Creon, the king?

ISMENE: No, Antigone, I haven't heard any news, good or bad. I have not heard anything since we lost our two brothers, who killed one another in battle.

ANTIGONE: Ah, yes. I thought you had not heard. That is why I asked you to come outside the palace gates so that I could talk to you privately.

ISMENE: So tell me what you are talking about.

ANTIGONE: It is about our Uncle Creon and our poor brothers. Eteocles has been properly buried and read his funeral rites. But our uncle has decreed that Polyneices, who also died in battle, may not be buried. Whoever disobeys our uncle's law will be put to death.

ISMENE: What are you suggesting we do?

ANTIGONE: Are you willing to join me in my mission? It is dangerous.

ISMENE: Antigone, you must tell me what you are planning to do.

ANTIGONE: Are you willing to help me bury our brother?

ISMENE: And go against our uncle's decree?

ANTIGONE: Polyneices is still my brother and yours, too. I will not desert him.

ISMENE: You are very daring to do such a thing when you know our uncle has forbidden it.

ANTIGONE: What right does our uncle have to keep us from our own brother?

ISMENE: Oh, sister, please remember how our father died because of evil he brought upon himself. And now our brothers are gone. We are the only two left. It would be terrible if we both died because we broke this law. We must obey our uncle. It is not wise to act in this manner.

ANTIGONE: Do what you want. I will go bury my brother, and if I have to die because of it, then so be it.

ISMENE: I am too weak to fight our uncle. But I am very afraid for you. Do not tell anyone what you are doing. I will keep your secret.

© Harcourt

ACT 2

(*The Chorus enters King Creon's palace. They are singing a song of praise that the battle has ended. They also sing of the battle, including the deaths of Eteocles and Polyneices. After they have finished singing, Creon, the new King of Thebes, enters to address them.*)

CREON: My friends, I have called you here today to talk to you about what has happened. The gods are smiling on us, and we have overcome our recent troubles. I know that you were faithful when Oedipus, my brother, was king. And now, Oedipus's sons, Eteocles and Polyneices, have both died in combat with each other. Because I am family, I will now take over the throne. I promise to protect you, my subjects. I have honored Eteocles because he fought bravely for us, but I condemn the acts of Polyneices, who fought against us. I have decreed that he must not be buried, and whoever disobeys me will be put to death.

CHORUS MEMBER 1: We understand, King Creon. And we know that you have the power to make the rules that govern both the living and the dead.

CREON: You must make sure that my orders are carried out.

CHORUS MEMBER 2: You must ask a younger man to do the job.

CREON: I have already appointed guards to watch the body of Polyneices.

CHORUS MEMBER 1: What then would you like us to do?

CREON: Make sure that no one disobeys me.

CHORUS MEMBER 2: No one would be crazy enough to disobey you. It would mean death.

GUARD:	(*Enter Guard looking down at the ground nervously*) King Creon, I did not want you to hear the news from someone else, so here I am.
CREON:	What is it? Why are you so upset?
GUARD:	I will tell you, but first you must know that I did not do it, and I do not know who did.
CREON:	Say what you came to say and then go in peace.
GUARD:	I will speak. The body of Polyneices—someone has sprinkled dirt on it, trying to bury it.
CREON:	(*gasps*) What? Who would dare disobey me?
GUARD:	I do not know. There was no shovel, and the ground has not been dug up at all. There were no wheel tracks in the dust, and whoever did this deed has left no trace. When the watchman showed us what had happened at dawn, we were all very shocked and upset. We guards fought among ourselves trying to figure out who had done it, yet no one ever confessed. Finally, we knew that someone must come tell you, and it was my unhappy task.
CHORUS MEMBER 1:	I think that perhaps there was a divine helper in this deed.
CREON:	(*to the Chorus members*) What a stupid thing to say! Next you'll say it was the gods' idea to bury Polyneices. Do the gods approve of men who do evil? (*speaking now to the guard*) No, it is men who are rebelling against me. These evil men have bribed my guards with money. Money can make men do much wrong. Well, whoever has done this will pay the price. You will find out who has done this and bring him to me. Or was it you who accepted silver as a bribe?
GUARD:	(*terrified*) May I speak, or should I just go?
CREON:	Can't you see how much your words upset me?
GUARD:	I did not do this. I did not take money to look the other way.
CREON:	That may be, but if you don't bring me the man who did this, you will pay the price for lying. (*Creon turns on his heel and storms out.*)
GUARD:	(*to the Chorus Members*) I hope the evildoer is found, but either way, I won't be coming here again. The gods have protected me here today.

THE END

UNIT 4 Simulations and Games

FACT OR FICTION   Divide the class into two groups. Make sure that students have pencils, index cards, and resource materials. Each group should generate a list of at least 20 statements about ancient Greece. Give students a time limit at the beginning of the game to keep them on task. Some of the statements they write should be factual, and some should be fictitious. Statements that are factual must be verifiable. Statements that are fictitious should not be so implausible that the answer is obvious. When both groups have completed their lists, it's time to play Fact or Fiction. Students from each group take turns reading a statement. The opponent must decide if the statement is fact or fiction. For example, "Homer is sometimes known as 'the Father of History.' Fact or fiction?" Encourage students not to give away the answer with their facial expressions. Keep score on the board. For every correct answer, a team wins a point, and for every incorrect answer, a team loses a point. The team with the most points at the end is the winner. *GAME*

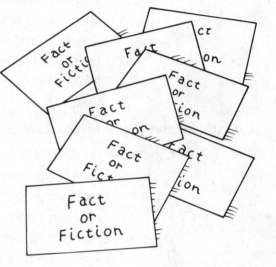

WORD SCRAMBLE   This game will test how well students know important terms from the unit. On the board, write scrambled versions of important terms from the unit. For a more challenging game, include only words that appear in bold in the unit. Students will use their own paper to try to unscramble the words as quickly as possible. Students should not use their textbooks to figure out the words. The first student to correctly unscramble all the words, or the most words within a specified time period, wins. If you would like to extend the game, when the majority of students have finished unscrambling words, suggest a new round. In this round, students will define the words as quickly as possible. *GAME*

POP-UP GREEKS Distribute index cards to each student. Using their knowledge of ancient Greece, students should write one or two questions and answers on the card. For variety, consider asking one side of the room to write about one portion of the unit and one group to write about another portion. Collect cards from students. Tell students that you will read a question from the cards. If a student knows the answer, he or she should "pop" up out of his or her seat and call out the answer. Ask students to sit out when the questions they have written are read. Play continues until all questions have been asked. *GAME*

DEBATE ON DEMOCRACY In this simulation, students will stage a mock debate between Cleisthenes and a congressional representative of today. Cleisthenes was an Athenian leader who made major changes in the way that Athens was governed. He championed a direct democracy in which each citizen participated directly in making decisions. Remind the students of how the United States functions as a representative democracy. Divide the class into two groups. One group will support Cleisthenes and a direct democracy, and one group will support a congressional representative of today and a representative democracy. Ask the class to prepare a simple debate (with multiple speakers) on the topic as if Cleisthenes and a modern politician were able to meet and compare forms of democracy. Have each side present an argument based on the pros and cons of each type of democracy. At the end of the debate, decide which side presented the more convincing argument. *SIMULATION*

Long-Term Project

A GUIDEBOOK TO GREEK THEATER

In this project, students will create a book about Greek Theater. At the end of the project, they will present the book as a comprehensive guide to the history of ancient playacting.

Week 1

👤👤👤 group   🕐 45 minutes

Materials: paper, pencils

Introduce the topic by asking students if they have ever participated in a play. Tell students that they will be creating a guidebook to ancient Greek theater. Each group will be assigned different parts of the book, and in Week 4, each group will make a presentation to the rest of the class. At the very end of the project, the book should be carefully bound together and kept as a valuable classroom resource.

Break the class into four groups and assign the following tasks: Group 1—create the front cover art and write an introduction to Greek theater; Group 2—diagram a Greek theater and write about the structure of Greek tragedies and comedies; Group 3—catalog Greek masks and costumes and write about famous Greek playwrights and their plays; Group 4—create back cover art and write about similarities between Greek theater and modern theater. Each group will produce one piece of art and one mini-report.

Suggest that each group brainstorm about their tasks. Emphasize that it is important for students to collect research materials and bring them in for Week 2.

Week 2

👤👤👤 group   🕐 45 minutes

Materials: paper, pencils, resource materials

This week, students should begin writing their mini-reports for the book. Next week, they may work on the artwork portion of the book. Decide the size of the book ahead of time so that students can plan accordingly. Students should review their research and write as much of the report as they can. For Week 3, the report can be typed or otherwise prepared to be mounted in the book.

Week 3

👥 group   🕐 45 minutes

Materials: craft paper, glue or tape, markers or paints and paintbrushes, construction paper, scissors

This week, students should work on creating the artwork for each section. Students may have pictures they wish to use, or they may create their own art. Group 1 should design the front cover of the book, group 2 should design a labeled diagram of the actual theater, group 3 should create a short catalogue of Greek masks and costumes, and group 4 should design the back cover of the book. If time allows, students may begin mounting their artwork on craft paper. Mounting on construction paper can add color to the pages.

Week 4

👥 group   🕐 45 minutes

Materials: mini-reports, artwork, any materials needed to finish the book

This week, students should put any necessary finishing touches on their portions of the book. Each piece of art and each mini-report should be mounted. When students have finished, start with Group 1, and have each group explain both their artwork and their mini-reports to the rest of the class. When all the groups have finished, bind the book together and keep it in the classroom as a resource.

Tips for combination classrooms:

 For grade five, students can research the beginning of American theater during the early nineteenth century.

 For grade seven, students can research the arts and theater during the Renaissance.

© Harcourt

These short-term projects give students exposure to various aspects of ancient Greece. Students can design posters about the Cyclades Islands or the first Olympics, learn to speak like Socrates, and so on.

Travel to the Cyclades

👥 partners   🕐 40 minutes

Materials: posterboard, colored pencils or markers, resource materials

The Cyclades Islands are located in the Aegean Sea. There are about 200 islands in all. Because the climate is mild and the scenery is beautiful, the islands are a popular vacation spot for tourists. Break students into pairs and ask each pair to imagine that they are designing a poster for the window of a travel agency. The poster should highlight reasons why people might want to visit the Cyclades Islands. Students may need briefly to do some additional research on the Cyclades. Encourage students to use vivid colors to make their posters appealing. Display students' artwork when the projects are finished.

Answer Like Socrates

👥 partners   🕐 20 minutes

Materials: paper, pencils

One of the world's best known philosophers was Socrates. He was famous for answering questions by asking other questions. His goal was to get people he spoke with to really think about issues. Break the class into pairs and give each pair a question. Sample questions could include: What is truth? What is freedom? What is courage? Students must then conduct conversations with each other in the manner of Socrates. Each student must speak using only questions. Ask students to pay attention to what they say and try to record the answer to the original question. Students should also note the other issues raised as they try to answer questions by asking questions.

© Harcourt

The Hippocratic Oath

small group   40 minutes

Materials: posterboard, markers, resource materials

Hippocrates was a Greek doctor who is best remembered for drafting the Hippocratic Oath. The Hippocratic Oath is a promise, or pledge, that lays down guidelines for the behavior of doctors. Doctors still take this oath today when they graduate from medical school. Break your students into small groups and ask each group to find a modern version of the Hippocratic Oath. (It is easily found online.) The modern version may be easier for students to understand than the classical, but either will do for this project. Using the posterboard and markers, students should make a list of the promises a doctor makes in the oath. Tell students that they must use their own words. Invite the groups to compare their completed lists and look for differences in interpretation.

The First Olympics

small group   40 minutes

Materials: posterboard, markers or paints, paintbrushes, resource materials

The Olympic Games have a rich history in Greece. Beginning around 776 B.C., athletes from each of the Greek city-states competed in different athletic events. City-states would lay aside their differences for the duration of the games. Break students into small groups and ask each group to make a poster celebrating the ancient Olympic Games. Students may consult resource materials for ideas. Posters may highlight certain events, or they may be more general. Students should attempt to get into the spirit of the ancient games and try to ignore modern symbols of the Olympics. Make sure that each member of the group participates in making the poster. When groups have finished, display each group's artwork in the classroom.

© Harcourt

Writing Projects

These prompts allow students to write both creatively and academically as they delve deeper into different facets of ancient Greece.

A Minoan Web Page

Historians have collected lots of information about how the Minoans lived, but they are still mystified by the Minoan culture's disappearance. Challenge students to design and write a Web page about the Minoan people, their way of life, and their disappearance. The Web page may contain small pieces of art, but the focus should be on communicating information about the Minoans. Remind students that Web pages are different from encyclopedia articles. Information must be very clear and well organized so that the site is attractive and easy to use.

A Greek Guidebook to Gods and Goddesses

The people of Greece believed in an array of gods and goddesses. Each deity had different powers and could affect anything from the weather, to the oceans, to relationships between people. Ask students to make a "Top Ten" guidebook to Greek gods and goddesses. Students should find their favorite Greek gods and goddesses and write short entries about each of them. The guidebook should start with a short introduction.

Fashion Your Own Fable

There is no more famous writer of fables than Aesop. His stories were more than entertainment; they were teaching tools. And they continue to be read and interpreted today. Have students review a short fable, and then ask them to write their own fables. The fable should end with a moral. To get students started, you may choose to provide everyone with the same moral. For example, students could write fables that illustrate the moral "Cheaters never prosper." Encourage students to use animal characters and simple scenarios to create their fables.

© Harcourt

A Letter Home

Spartan children were educated at Spartan training camps. At the age of seven, children were sent to the camps to learn how to become responsible and valuable Spartan citizens. Ask students to review what they know about Spartan training and education. Then invite them to imagine that they are Spartan children. Have each student write a letter home, describing a typical day at Camp Sparta. Encourage students to make use of sensory detail in their letters. Remind students that being a citizen of Sparta was a very high honor.

Agree or Disagree?

Pericles, a Greek leader and general, made the following statement about freedom: "Freedom is the sure possession of those alone who have the courage to defend it." Ask students to write a persuasive essay in which they agree or disagree with Pericles's statement. First, students should explain what they think the statement means. Then students should decide whether they agree or disagree with it. Advise students to express their opinions clearly and logically, and to use examples to strengthen their arguments.

History Makers

The Greeks made numerous contributions to science, history, medicine, mathematics, philosophy, and art. Even today, many of the great Greek thinkers are remembered for their work. Ask each student to choose his or her favorite Greek thinker to make the subject of a short biography. Students may choose to write about Pythagoras, Hippocrates, or Democritus, to name only a few important figures. Challenge students to include a paragraph on whether the contribution of the figure they chose is still meaningful in today's modern world. Why or why not?

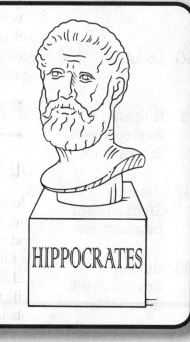
HIPPOCRATES

4 Daily Geography

1. **Location**   On which peninsula is present-day Greece located?

2. **Place**   What is a peninsula?

3. **Place**   Which three bodies of water surround the Balkan Peninsula?

4. **Regions**   Which present-day country covers much of the region once called Asia Minor?

5. **Place**   What connects the southern part of Greece, called the Peloponnesus, to the rest of Greece?

6. **Place**   Which kind of landform covers most of Greece?

7. **Location**   What is the largest of the Greek islands called?

8. **Human-Environment Interactions**   Greece's dry climate and rocky soil caused early farmers to grow which of the following crops?
   corn and wheat
   rice and beans
   olives, grapes, and barley

9. **Movement**   Which method of travel did the early Greeks use because it was easier than crossing the mountains?

10. **Location**   Which group of about 200 islands is located east of the Greek mainland?

11. **Human-Environment Interactions**   Who probably introduced the Greeks to the written alphabet?

12. **Human-Environment Interactions**   Which civilization developed on the island of Crete?

13. **Human-Environment Interactions**   What is unique about the Minoan clay tablets that have survived to this day?

© Harcourt

14. Location   Around 1200 B.C., the Mycenaeans conquered a city called Troy. Where was Troy located?

15. Location   What are the names of Greece's two best-known city-states?

16. Place   Which natural barriers separated many of the Greek city-states, causing them to develop independently of one another?

17. Regions   By 500 B.C., the Greeks had founded colonies in which parts of the world?

18. Location   Where did the first Olympic Games take place?

19. Location   How did the location of Athens encourage trade?

20. Regions   From what region did the Persians rule?

21. Regions   By 400 B.C., how far reaching were the borders of the Persian Empire?

22. Location   In a rebellion in 499 B.C., Greek colonists burned the western capital of the Persian Empire. What was the name of that capital?

23. Location   To defend themselves against attack by Xerxes, the Athenian navy waited quietly between the Greek coastline and which island?

24. Human-Environment Interactions   What is the name of the temple the Greeks built to honor the goddess Athena?

25. Human-Environment Interactions   Which human-made system of defense connected the city of Athens to the port of Piraeus?

26. Location   In which Greek city-state did an exiled Athenian general form an army in hopes of winning back Athens from Sparta?

27. Location   Which three city-states formed the Corinthian Alliance?

28. Regions   Where was Macedonia, home of King Philip II, located?

29. Movement   To complete his father's plan to rule Persia and the rest of the world, Alexander and his troops entered Asia Minor in 334 B.C. Which path did Alexander follow before taking over the Persian Empire in 330 B.C.?

30. Location   Which Egyptian city rivaled Athens as the center of Greek culture and learning?

Why Character Counts

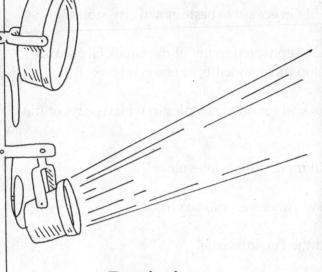

- **Trustworthiness**
- **Respect**
- **Responsibility**
- **Fairness**
- **Caring**
- ## Patriotism

Patriotism

Patriotism is defined as love or devotion to your country. Patriotism can also mean having feelings of pride in your country. People can show patriotism in very different ways. Citizens on opposite sides of an issue may disagree about what is best for their country, but both sides may be equally patriotic.

At a very early age, Spartan children began learning the meaning of patriotism. The children attended training camps where they learned to defend their beloved city-state. Children were taught to have great pride and love for Sparta. A Spartan citizen believed that the greatest gift a person could give to Sparta was to sacrifice his or her life for it.

In your own words:

Write a definition for the word *patriotism*.

_____

_____

_____

_____

© Harcourt

Name _____

Character Activity

Do you think that patriotism is an important part of a person's character? Give reasons for your answer. Write a short essay in which you explain why you think that patriotism is an important part of a person's character. At the conclusion of the essay, include ways that you can express your own feelings of patriotism.

_____

_____

_____

_____

_____

_____

_____

_____

_____

_____

_____

_____

_____

_____

_____

UNIT 4 Economic Literacy

Supply and Demand

Have you heard the terms *supply* and *demand*? Even if you are not sure what those terms mean, you have probably heard them before. Supply and demand are two of the most basic economic principles. Supply is the amount of something that a company has to sell. For example, if a company has 20,000 pairs of denim jeans to sell, the supply is 20,000. Demand is the amount of something that the buyer wants to buy. If 21,000 people want to purchase denim jeans, then the demand is 21,000, and the demand exceeds the supply. If only 15,000 people want to purchase the jeans, then the supply is greater than the demand. When supply equals demand, there is an equilibrium, or balance.

What does all this mean to you? As a customer, you are interested in the price of items that you want to buy. The law of supply and demand is what drives the price of an item. Let us go back to the example in the first paragraph. If 21,000 people want jeans, but there are only 20,000 pairs available, the supplier knows that he or she can offer the jeans for a higher price than if only 15,000 people wanted the jeans. If only 15,000 people want to buy a certain kind of jeans, then the supplier is likely to put the jeans on sale to try to get people to buy more of them.

A similar principle was applied in ancient Greece as city-states began to make trade agreements with each other. In order to be successful at trading, a city-state would have to offer a product for which there was already a demand. Otherwise, there was no need for a trade. Other factors also affect the value or price of goods. If a product takes a long time to make, or if moving the product from one place to another is costly, the price or value of an item will be greater.

Supply and Demand Activity

Think about things that you or your parents buy regularly. What items are always in high demand? Do these items ever go on sale? Are there times when one item is in higher demand than another?

_____

_____

_____

_____

_____

Think about new cars that are for sale. What is the effect on the price of a car when the demand is low? What sorts of things could a supplier do to create a higher demand for an item?

_____

_____

_____

_____

_____

_____

_____

UNIT 4 Citizenship

Read About It One of the ideals that Americans hold most dear is the concept of equality. Equality for all citizens of the United States has evolved over time. The process began with the Declaration of Independence, signed July, 4, 1776, which contains the famous words, "We hold these truths to be self-evident, that all men are created equal . . ." At the time, the words applied only to white male citizens, but today we interpret those words to mean equality for everyone. The Thirteenth Amendment, passed in 1865, officially abolished slavery, and the Fourteenth Amendment, passed in 1868, guaranteed every citizen the same rights and protection under the law. Equality for all United States citizens did not happen overnight, but in the eyes of the government and the law, every person is now equal.

1. What does the word *equality* mean to you as an American citizen?

_____

_____

_____

2. Why do you think the Declaration of Independence only recognized male citizens as being created equal?

_____

_____

_____

© Harcourt

Name _____

Talk About It   Are there still barriers to real equality in the United States? If so, what are they? Is each person truly equal in American society? Are there some people who still seem to be treated differently from others? Why do you think that is?

Write About It   In the 500s B.C., Solon, a respected leader in Athens, took key steps toward achieving equality in Athenian society. What did Solon do to solve a crisis in Athens? What other reforms did Solon make that affected the way people in Athens participated in government? Write an essay in which you answer these questions. Make sure to support your essay with examples.

_____

_____

_____

_____

_____

_____

_____

_____

_____

_____

_____

_____

_____

© Harcourt

Map Envelopes
Unit 5

Materials needed:

*Two stick-on address labels

*Outline maps of India and
 China

*Scissors

*Glue stick

*Markers or colored pencils

*Sheets of drawing paper

Social Studies Skills:

*World Geography

*India

*China

Reading Skills:

*Main Idea and Details

*Generalize

Instructions:

1. Make one map envelope at a
   time. Color in the map and fold
   it into three sections. Make the
   middle and bottom sections
   equal in size and the top about 1
   inch shorter.

2. Unfold and fold the sides in
   about 2 inches.

Illustrations:

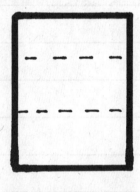

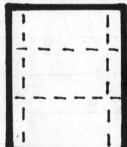

3. Cut away the side flaps from the bottom and top sections, leaving them only on the middle section. Cut the top section diagonally to form the envelope closure.

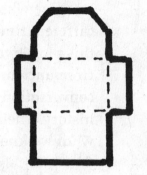

4. Refold the map and glue it to form an envelope. Add the stick-on label to the front, and write the title of the chapter on it. Repeat steps 1-4 for the other map.

5. Use the drawing paper to create a review sheet for each lesson of the chapter. Write and illustrate the main ideas and details.

6. Fold completed review sheets and place in the map envelopes for later use.

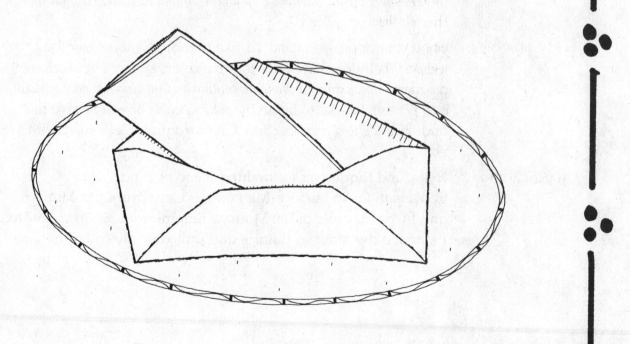

CONVERSATIONS IN HISTORY

Imagine what it would be like if leaders of the world from different time periods could meet to discuss their ideas. In this play, two leaders from ancient India and two leaders from ancient China meet for a discussion. While the conversation is imaginary, the people are real figures from history. Their answers to the questions are consistent with what we know about their leadership styles.

Cast of Characters

- Chandragupta Maurya, *ruler of the Maurya Empire*
  320 B.C. – 297 B.C. *(India)*
- Ashoka, *ruler of the Maurya Empire*
  273 B.C – 232 B.C. *(India)*
- King Wu, *ruler of the Zhou dynasty (China)*
- Shi Huangdi, *ruler of the Qin dynasty (China)*
- Ms. Histoire, *the moderator*

[*Ms. Histoire sits at the head of a long rectangular table. Around the table sit the four rulers.*]

MS. HISTOIRE: Good afternoon, everyone. I'd like to thank you for coming today. It is indeed an honor to have rulers such as yourselves as guests (*looks around the table smiling and making eye contact with each person*). I'd like to begin by asking each of you to give the audience a short introduction. Chandragupta, let's start with you.

CHANDRAGUPTA: Hello, and thank you for inviting me to be a part of Conversations in History. My name is Chandragupta Maurya, and I was the ruler of the Maurya Empire from 320 B.C. – 297 B.C. I founded the Maurya Empire and united northern India.

© Harcourt

ASHOKA:	Hello, I am Ashoka. I, too, ruled the Maurya Empire in India, and I began my rule much in the same way as Chandragupta, but I ended it very differently.
MS. HISTOIRE:	Yes, thank you. We'll get to some of those differences shortly. And now, King Wu, would you introduce yourself?
KING WU:	(*nodding*) Yes, of course. I am King Wu. I ruled the Zhou dynasty in China. I defeated the Shang dynasty in 1050 B.C., and my conquest marked the beginning of the Zhou dynasty.
SHI HUANGDI:	I am Shi Huangdi. I took the throne when I was only 13 years old. I was known as the First Emperor of China. In the beginning, I ruled with the help of Li Si, one of my top government officials.
MS. HISTOIRE:	Wonderful. Now that we know a little about all of you, I'd like to ask some questions about your leadership style, your philosophies, and the people over whom you ruled. My first question is for Chandragupta. What were some of the things you did to organize the Indian empire after you took power?
CHANDRAGUPTA:	Yes, well, I prided myself on my organization. To me it was very important to know what the people in my empire were doing. I was able to create more farmland in India, and I was also responsible for improving the roads of the empire.
MS. HISTOIRE:	How did you finance your projects?
CHANDRAGUPTA:	Ah, yes. You must have money to carry out projects like the ones I wanted to undertake. I felt that the people of my empire should pay heavy taxes to cover the expenses of my projects. The projects benefited everyone, so everyone was required to contribute.
SHI HUANGDI:	I felt taxes were very important as well. I also felt that it was important that the taxes go directly to me, rather than go through the feudal lords first. I trusted very few people.
CHANDRAGUPTA:	That's a very important point. A ruler must maintain complete control. He cannot trust most people.

© Harcourt

MS. HISTOIRE:	Let's talk about that for a minute. Chandragupta, did you have a particular philosophy of leadership?
CHANDRAGUPTA:	I did. I read a very important book called *Arthashastra*. One of the few advisors I trusted recommended the book to me. The book talks about how you must use punishment and war to get ahead in leadership.
MS. HISTOIRE:	(*raising her eyebrows and looking very surprised*) Punishment and war?
CHANDRAGUPTA:	Yes, and you can see how well my ideas worked. I was able to expand the Maurya Empire across most of northern India. I was a very successful ruler.
MS. HISTOIRE:	(*annoyed*) Yes, well, we'll talk about that in a minute. In the meantime, King Wu, perhaps you can tell us how you came to power.
KING WU:	Certainly. I came to power because of the Mandate of Heaven.
MS. HISTOIRE:	Can you tell us more about that, please?
KING WU:	The Zhou people, my people, worshipped the god Tian. Tian gave me the strength to defeat the Shang dynasty and take over as ruler. The Shang rulers were cruel to their people, and they deceived them. A ruler must show more virtue than that to be allowed to stay in power.
MS. HISTOIRE:	And what is the Mandate of Heaven?
KING WU:	The Mandate of Heaven is from our god Tian. It says that as long as I, or any other Zhou authority, show the qualities of virtue, we will be allowed to stay in power. But, if I become greedy, or if I decide to treat my people unkindly, then Tian will not allow me to continue to rule.
ASHOKA:	Please, I must speak. At first, I was very much like Chandragupta. I was fierce in battle, and I was able to extend my kingdom even farther than his kingdom. I was cruel to my people, and I was overcome by my own power. But then something happened, and I was forever changed.
MS. HISTOIRE:	Please tell us about it. What happened?

ASHOKA: It was in 261 B.C. that I defeated the kingdom of Kalinga. But at such a price! I looked out over the battlefield, and I did not feel victory. I felt terrible sadness and regret. Many, many thousands of people died in that battle. It was a terrible waste.

SHI HUANGDI: You cannot avoid loss of life in war. Only a weak ruler would worry about that.

MS. HISTOIRE: But Shi Huangdi, weren't you terribly afraid of dying yourself? You built an enormous tomb and had at least 7,000 life-size clay soldiers made to be buried in your tomb. Some people have said that you cared more about preserving your own life than anything else.

SHI HUANGDI: (*looking annoyed*) I was very important to the Qin people. I am responsible for legalism and standardization. These were my major achievements. I am also very proud of the long wall I built.

KING WU: But if you rule your people without kindness, you will not be great. A man who is cruel is great in his own eyes only.

CHANDRAGUPTA: That's ridiculous. You must control the people and not allow them to think they are better than you. The ruling class of my empire did not suffer. Only the common people did not appreciate me.

ASHOKA: Perhaps that is because they were overtaxed and overworked. You were greatly disliked, Chandragupta. And you knew that, because you feared assassination. You feared it so much that you slept in a different room every night. That is not the mark of a strong man. That is the mark of a fearful man.

CHANDRAGUPTA: You were weak, Ashoka. You allowed yourself to be influenced by Buddha. You forgot that being a ruler means making choices that your people may not like.

KING WU: You are wrong, Chandragupta. The hardest choice is for peace, and that is the path that Ashoka chose.

MS. HISTOIRE: (*a little uneasy*) Gentlemen, I want to thank you for coming today, but I'm afraid we're out of time. But I think our audience has learned a lot today about different types of leadership. I know I have a better picture of each of you now. Perhaps the question we should all leave with is this: Which is the bigger victory—conquest or virtue? Thank you all.

THE END

Simulations and Games

MAKE YOUR OWN WORD SEARCH To play this game students will need graph paper and pencils. Write the following words on the board: CITADEL, PAKISTAN, DECCAN, HARAPPA, CASTE, PUNJAB, NIRVANA, THE BUDDHA, ASHOKA, MONSOON, VEDAS, STEPPE, YANGTZE, DIALECT, SILKWORM, VIRTUE, FEUDALISM, SHANG, ZHOU, LEGALISM. Tell students that they will each be making a word search game. Students should draw a box of fifteen-by-fifteen squares on the graph paper. They should then write the words for the word search game on the grid. Set ground rules that determine how words can be listed (i.e. diagonally, horizontally, vertically, and reversed). Students should fill in the remaining empty boxes with other letters from the alphabet. All letters should be uppercase. Once students have completed their word searches, they should trade with classmates and play the game. As they play, invite students to the board to define the words. The first student to hand in a completed word search wins. However, all words must be defined before any word searches are handed in. *GAME*

DESCRIBE IT! This is a revised version of a popular game. You will need a stopwatch to play this game. Divide the class into two teams. Give each team a set of ten to fifteen index cards. Have each team write a word or phrase related to either ancient India or ancient China on each of the cards. Then have students sit in a circle. No two members of the same team should sit next to one another. Now you are ready to begin play. Give a student from one team the complete stack of shuffled index cards. The person holding the cards will look only at the top card. He or she will then use words and possibly gestures to try to make team members guess the correct word or phrase. As soon as the team guesses the word or phrase, the stack of cards should be quickly passed to the person on the right, who will look at the next card and try to describe the word or phrase for his or her team. Time each round at 60–90 seconds. The team that is *not* left holding the cards at the end of each round gets a point. Play until all the cards have been used or to a predetermined number of points. *GAME*

HOW MANY WORDS?

This game will reinforce unit content and test students' abilities to work under pressure. The game can be played in teams or individually. Using the following list of words, write one word (or group of words) at a time on the board: SUBCONTINENT, BANGLADESH, MOHENJO-DARO, MESOPOTAMIA, REINCARNATION, BHAGAVAD GITA, MOHANDAS GHANDI, ENLIGHTENMENT, CHANDRAGUPTA MAURYA, AFGHANISTAN, CHANG JIANG VALLEY, MANDATE OF HEAVEN, CONFUCIANISM, ORACLE BONE, SHI HUANGDI, BUREAUCRACY, STANDARDIZATION, SILK ROAD. Using their own paper and pencils, students should try to make as many smaller words as they can from the letters of each word on the board. Set a time limit for each round. When time has expired, the student who has been able to make the most words gets a point. (The student should read his or her list aloud.) Award an extra point to the student if he or she can offer meaningful information about the word on the board. If the student cannot add information, let the first student who raises his or her hand try to get a point. Play until all the words have been exhausted. *GAME*

CITY PLANNERS

The cities in the Indus River valley were very well planned and surprisingly intricate in their design. In this simulation students will have the opportunity to help plan a city such as Harappa or Mohenjo-Daro. Divide the class into two or four groups. Each team will be responsible for designing plans for a city in the Indus River valley. Tell students they must devise a plan and present it to city leaders. They will be competing with the other groups to present the best plan. Students should consider what buildings they will include in their city plan, as well as the physical layout of the city. Students should spend time writing and designing a plan and then present their plans to the rest of the class. Take a vote at the end to see which set of plans was the most comprehensive. *SIMULATION*

5 Long-Term Project

EAST AND WEST: A COMPARATIVE STUDY

With this project, students can enhance their understanding of the early civilizations of India and China while comparing them to early settlements in the United States.

| Week 1 | 👥👥 group | 🕐 45 minutes |

Materials: paper, pencils

Introduce the topic by asking students if they think the ancient civilizations in India and China could have anything in common with the United States. Ask students for predictions about what they think they will find when they compare two vastly different cultures on opposite sides of the world.

Break the class into two groups—India and China. Each group will create a separate display and present their findings during Week 4. For the group assigned to India, students may wish to compare the Maurya Empire under Ashoka with the early Jamestown settlement. For the group assigned to China, students may wish to compare the Zhou or Qin dynasties with the Plymouth settlement.

Explain to students that they must create a three-paneled display. The two outer panels should contain pictures and drawings of the two places being compared. A map of each place should be included. The center panel should consist of a comparison—in essay or chart form—of the two places. Topics may include the following: geography, government, role of religion, and so on. Students should meet to discuss how they will approach the project and divide the tasks among themselves. Outside of class, students should do research on their displays and bring their findings and visual materials to class the following week.

© Harcourt

Week 2

 group   ⏱ 45 minutes

Materials: posterboard, glue, scissors, markers, tape, resource materials

This week students should begin creating their displays using the materials (images, maps, etc.) that they have brought to class. Students may begin assembling the two outer panels of the display. One side should depict images, drawings, and maps of either India or China, and the other side of the display should depict the same type of information about either Jamestown or Plymouth. Between Weeks 2 and 3, students should complete the research necessary for their comparative study and bring the research to class with them next week.

Week 3

👥 group   ⏱ 45 minutes

Materials: posterboard, markers, glue, scissors, resource materials

This week students should finish any remaining work on the outer panels of their displays and begin work on the center panels. Students should come up with an attractive, eye-catching way of displaying the information about the places they have studied. Students may arrange the information in any way that is clear and that addresses the topics for their group.

Week 4

👥 group   ⏱ 45 minutes

Materials: completed displays

This week students should quickly put any necessary finishing touches on their displays and be ready to present the information to the rest of the class. Each group should take turns telling the class about their research. Students should also explain the pictures, drawings, and maps that they used on the outer panels.

Tips for combination classrooms:

5–6 For grade five, include information about early Colonial settlements.

6–7 For grade seven, consider discussing medieval Japan and medieval Europe.

UNIT 5 — Short-Term Projects

These short-term projects allow students to investigate India and China—both philosophically and artistically.

Ancient Harappan Seals

👤 individual   🕐 40 minutes

Materials: modeling clay, stylus or pen for marking, string, resource materials

Harappan seals were used in India for both local and foreign trade. They appear to have been marks of ownership or origin. The seals were made from steatite, a soft stone that was fired for hardness. They were hung on a cord and then placed on the goods. First, have students research these seals in the library or on the Internet. Ask them to find out what types of pictures were normally on the seals and the shape of the seals. Then students can fashion their own Harappan seals using the modeling clay and stylus. Students should try to imitate the style of the Harappan seals they were able to find in their research. Students should make a handle (called a *boss*) on the back of the seal so that the seal can be hung on the string. Display the students' seals once they are finished.

Exploring the *Bhagavad Gita*

👥 partners   🕐 20 minutes

Materials: paper, pencils, resource materials

The *Mahabharata,* a story from ancient India, is the longest epic poem ever written. One of the most famous and most often quoted parts of the *Mahabharata* is the *Bhagavad Gita.* Read the following lines from the ancient poem and then ask student pairs to interpret the meaning. *"Find full reward of doing right in right! Let right deeds be thy motive, not the fruit which comes from them. And live in action! Labor! Make thine acts thy piety, casting all self aside . . ."* Students may make notes if they wish. Ask students to share their insights about the message of these lines. If you wish, make a list of student observations on the board.

© Harcourt

An Army of Faces

👤 individual   🕐 30 minutes

Materials: drawing paper, colored pencils, resource materials

One of the most amazing archaeological finds in China is the tomb of Shi Huangdi. In it, archaeologists have found an entire army of soldiers made from clay. More than 7,000 life-size soldiers have been discovered, and they are unique in that no two are alike. Have students locate a few pictures of this unusual army and then ask them to draw a picture of what they see. The challenge is that while the uniforms of the soldiers may be the same, each of the faces must be different. Ask students to imagine what it must have been like to try to have 7,000 different faces represented in the clay army. Students should draw as many figures on their drawing paper as they can. Challenge students to explain what they have drawn by writing a short description of Shi Huangdi.

Illustrating Confucius

👥👥👥 small group   🕐 40 minutes

Materials: drawing paper, markers or colored pencils

Confucius is known for the many wise proverbs that he wrote. Break students into small groups, no more than three or four students per group. Give each group a different proverb from Confucius and ask the group to come up with a way to represent the meaning of the proverb in a picture. Groups should agree on the best way to illustrate the proverb. Students may use contemporary examples in their pictures. After the pictures have been drawn, ask each group to share their artwork and explain its meaning. Sample proverbs could include:
1) "Everything has its beauty, but not everyone sees it." 2) "Our greatest glory is not in never falling, but in rising every time we fall." 3) "Look for an occupation that you like, and you will not need to labor for a single day in your life." 4) "Wherever you go, go with all your heart." 5) "To know what is right and not do it is the worst cowardice."

These writing prompts encourage students to delve more deeply into history as they travel back in time to imagine, evaluate, compare, and understand.

A Farmer's Eye View

People in the Indus River valley were subjected to tremendous flooding each year as the summer monsoons caused the Indus River to swell and overflow its banks. Have students imagine that they are early farmers in the Indus River valley. Ask them to write a few descriptive paragraphs about the onset of the summer monsoons and the flooding that followed. Encourage students to use all five senses in their writing. Students should describe the physical effects of the monsoons and flooding, as well as the challenges that faced the farmers.

Classes and Castes

Around 1000 B.C., the Aryan society was divided into four main classes of people. Within each of these four classes of people were castes—further divisions of people based on their social standing. A person's caste determined what role he or she could play in Aryan society. Have students write an expository essay where they examine the Aryan view of society as parts of the human body. What benefits could come from such a view? Was there logic in the way the classes were assigned as different parts of the body? What problems could arise from such a view? Ask students to include their thoughts on why discrimination against people based on their castes is illegal in India today.

Comparison Chart of Indian Religions

Hinduism, Buddhism, and Jainism are three ancient religions with their roots in India. Have students prepare a compare/contrast chart of the basic similarities and differences among the three religions. Include information such as approximate date of origin, beliefs in deities, views on society, social behavior, and so on.

© Harcourt

A Turning Point

As a young man, Ashoka was harsh and cruel as a leader. Later, after looking at the thousands that had died in the battle to defeat Kalinga, he experienced a turning point in his life. He changed his ways and became a man of peace. He made many changes in the way that he ruled the Maurya Empire. Ask students to imagine that they are Emperor Ashoka and they are looking out at the battlefield after Kalinga has been defeated. Ask students to try to imagine the change that must have been going on inside Ashoka as he looked at the results of the bloody battle. Challenge students to write a journal entry that describes what Ashoka may have been thinking and feeling that day.

Think About It

After Shi Huangdi had introduced legalism, he also instituted standardization in many different areas. The provinces that Shi Huangdi ruled used different systems of money, weights and measures, and writing. This made it difficult to communicate and to conduct trade. Because he wanted to unify the empire under his rule, Shi Huangdi standardized money, weights and measures, and writing. Shi Huangdi also standardized education. Ask students to write an analysis of Shi Huangdi's standardization of education. Were there any benefits to standardizing education? How did Shi Huangdi approach the standardizing of books for learning? How do Shi Huangdi's policies differ from the way education is approached in the United States today? Students should make sure that they support their opinions with examples and solid reasoning.

Interpreting Confucius

The proverbs of Confucius are written in the *Analects*. Ancient students studied the words of Confucius, although the ideas of Confucianism did not become popular until after Confucius died. Give students the following proverb from Confucius: "Those who know the truth are not up to those who love it; those who love the truth are not up to those who delight in it." Ask students to imagine they are writing an entry on "truth" in a philosophy book and have been asked to interpret this quote. Students should support their interpretations with examples.

Daily Geography

1. **Regions**	Which present-day countries make up the Indian subcontinent?
2. **Place**	What is a subcontinent?
3. **Place**	Which geographic feature separates the Indian subcontinent from the rest of Asia?
4. **Place**	Which bodies of water lie west and east of the Indian subcontinent?
5. **Regions**	The Indian subcontinent can be divided into which two major geographic regions?
6. **Place**	Which two great rivers lie in the northern plains of the Indian subcontinent?
7. **Place**	Into which body of water does the Indus River flow?
8. **Human-Environment Interactions**	Why did southern Asia's first civilization form in the Indus River valley?
9. **Movement**	What was the effect of the summer monsoons in the Indus River valley?
10. **Movement**	Which body of water would a traveler going from Sri Lanka to India's mainland have to cross?
11. **Location**	What were the names of three of the largest and most important cities in the Indus River valley?
12. **Movement**	Through which mountain range did the Aryans pass to get to the Indian subcontinent?
13. **Human-Environment Interactions**	Emperor Ashoka was able to extend the Maurya Empire as far as which three present-day countries?
14. **Location**	In 262 B.C., Ashoka experienced a sudden turning point in his life after seeing thousands lying dead following the defeat of what kingdom?

© Harcourt

15. **Place**   What is the present-day name of the island nation located south of the Indian subcontinent?

16. **Regions**   Which areas of India did the Gupta Empire include?

17. **Place**   Which two rivers in China helped shape the early civilizations that developed there?

18. **Place**   Which river in China was named for its color, which was caused by sandy soil mixing with its water?

19. **Regions**   Which large desert lies along China's northern border with Mongolia?

20. **Place**   What is another name for the Chang Jiang or "Long River"?

21. **Place**   North of the Himalayas is the largest and highest plateau in the world. What is its name?

22. **Place**   In northern China, there are tall mountains, deserts, and steppes. What are steppes?

23. **Regions**   Which region of China has the lowest-lying land?

24. **Regions**   Which two major geographic features were barriers to trade and travel in ancient China?

25. **Human-Environment Interactions**   Why did the people of China come to believe that they were the world's only civilization?

26. **Human-Environment Interactions**   What system of defense did Shi Huangdi order to be built?

27. **Human-Environment Interactions**   What unusual things did archaeologists find when they excavated Shi Huangdi's tomb in the 1970s?

28. **Place**   Which of the following cities was the capital of the Han dynasty?
Chang'an
Zhenghou
Xianyang

29. **Movement** Which religion spread from India to China?

30. **Place**   What was the name of the most traveled trade route from the ancient Han capital through Asia to the Mediterranean Sea?

Why Character Counts

- Respect
- Fairness
- Responsibility
- Patriotism
- **Caring**
- Trustworthiness

Caring

Caring is the genuine interest or concern you show toward someone else. Caring is not motivated by a selfish desire to improve your own position. Rather, it involves putting others first. You can show caring to family and friends, but you can also show it toward people you don't know.

Confucius believed that the way people treated each other was very important. He often stressed the importance of kindness, or caring, in his teachings. Confucius believed that good relationships among people helped to make Chinese society a better place. In this quote, Confucius offers advice for how people should treat one another: "Act with kindness, but do not exact gratitude." That means that people should treat one another with kindness without expecting thanks.

In your own words:

Write a definition for the word *caring*.

_____

_____

_____

© Harcourt

Character Activity

What are some ways that you see examples of caring in the world around you? Are there areas of American society or culture where you think people should be more caring? Is showing care for others difficult in today's world? Why or why not? Answer these questions in a short essay. Make sure you explain the reasons for your answers.

_____

_____

_____

_____

_____

_____

_____

_____

_____

_____

_____

_____

_____

_____

_____

_____

Economic Literacy

Goods and Services

Did you buy anything today? What about last weekend? Did you buy school supplies, a new coat, or a cheeseburger? Or did you go to the dentist, get a haircut, or mail a package at the post office? No matter what you purchased, you probably exchanged your money for goods or services. Goods are things that you buy that you can physically touch. For example, a bottle of water and a car are both examples of goods. Services are different from goods because a service isn't something you can hold in your hand. A service refers to work that you pay someone else to do for you. People who provide services include painters, mechanics, and doctors. People in these occupations all perform a job for someone else.

As consumers, we spend the money that we earn on goods and services. What we must decide is if the goods and services that we want to buy are worthwhile, or of a good value. There are different kinds of goods that we can choose from. Durable goods are things that we buy that last for a long time, for example, cars and washing machines. Durable goods are more expensive than nondurable goods. Nondurable goods are products that only last for a short period of time, for example, food, children's clothes, and cosmetics.

Many ancient peoples, including those who lived in India and China, made their living producing goods and services. In the beginning, people did not have a system of money, and they traded with each other for the things they needed. Later, people began to use money to buy things. People all over the world both then and now make their living producing either goods or services.

Name _____

Goods and Services Activity

Review the definitions of durable and
nondurable goods and answer the following
questions on the lines below. How should
the approach to buying these types of goods
be different? How would your financial
planning be different if you were buying
lunch at a fast-food restaurant as opposed
to a new bicycle?

_____

_____

_____

_____

_____

What are services that you and your family regularly pay for? How can things such as
going to a baseball game or going to the movies be considered services?

_____

_____

_____

_____

_____

_____

_____

© Harcourt

5 Citizenship

Read About It There are at least six federal equal employment opportunity (EEO) laws that protect individuals from unfair hiring practices, or job discrimination, in the United States. Title VII of the Civil Rights Act of 1964 created the Equal Employment Opportunity Commission. Title VII also made it illegal for employers to discriminate based on a person's race, color, religion, sex, or national origin. Other important federal laws include the Age Discrimination in Employment Act of 1967, which protects people who are 40 years of age and older. And under Title I and Title V of the Americans with Disabilities Act of 1990, employers may not refuse to hire qualified people on the basis of their disabilities.

Why do you think that laws about job discrimination had to be passed at the federal level? Why not leave the decision up to each individual state?

_____

_____

_____

Why do you think there had to be six different laws about job discrimination?

_____

_____

_____

© Harcourt

Name _____

Talk About It   Imagine a situation where a bookstore owner refuses to hire anyone who does not have a high school diploma. That means that high school students looking for summer jobs would not be hired because of their age and level of education. Is this fair? Is it job discrimination? Why or why not?

Write About It   Around 1000 B.C., the Aryan culture in India had four basic social classes, and within those classes a caste system developed. How did the caste system affect the job a person could hold? Do you think there are any situations in the United States today that are like the former Indian caste system? Do you think that the employment opportunities in the United States are truly equal? Write an essay in which you answer these questions. Think carefully about your response, and make sure to support your essay with examples.

_____

_____

_____

_____

_____

_____

_____

_____

_____

_____

_____

_____

CD
Accordian-Style
Unit 6

Materials needed:

*Empty plastic CD jewel case

*Sheets of drawing paper

*Glue or tape

*Markers or colored pencils

*Scissors

*Drawing compass

Social Studies Skills:

*Ancient Rome

*Historical Background

*Government

Reading Skills:

*Summarize

*Generalize

*Categorize

Instructions:

1. Using the drawing compass, create and cut out four CD-size circles out of drawing paper. Overlap them slightly and glue or tape them together to form a chain of CDs.

2. Draw, outline, and color in pictures on the CDs that show facts about ancient Rome. Make the first CD the cover, and give it a title. Then use the center portion of the CD to write information.

Illustration:

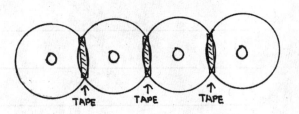

© Harcourt

3. Fold the CDs accordian-style to form
a booklet.

4. Lay the booklet in the CD jewel case
so that by pulling on the front CD, the
booklet can be read.

THE ANCIENT ROME CLUB

The ancient Rome Club in this play is a group that meets to discuss Roman history. In this performance, two scholars have come to a meeting to teach the group about ancient Rome. Join in as the group discusses mythology and reads aloud the story of Daedalus and Icarus.

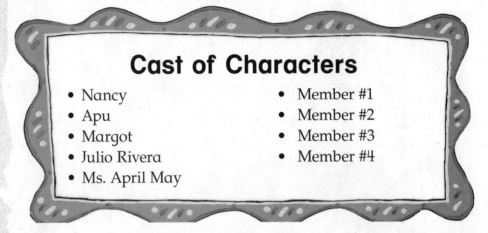

Cast of Characters

- Nancy
- Apu
- Margot
- Julio Rivera
- Ms. April May

- Member #1
- Member #2
- Member #3
- Member #4

[*Seven members of the Ancient Rome Club sit at a long table. Among them are team leaders, Apu and Margot, and Nancy, the club president. Also present are two scholars of Roman history.*]

NANCY: Good afternoon and welcome to the first ever experts' meeting of the Ancient Rome Club, or the ARC. As you know, today is a very special day. We're going to learn from two scholars who study different topics about ancient Rome. Apu, have you prepared your introduction?

APU: Yes, of course.

NANCY: Please welcome our first guest.

APU: As we all know, Greek myths inspired Latin poets, who used poetry to retell myths. My guest is an expert on mythology. Please welcome Mr. Julio Rivera, who will lead us in reading an adaptation of the myth of Icarus and Daedalus, made famous by the Latin poet Ovid.

JULIO RIVERA: Thank you, Apu. Before we begin our reading, let me tell you a bit about Ovid. Do any of you know about his life?

MEMBER #4: He was banished from Rome. And he lived after another Latin poet named Virgil.

JULIO RIVERA: That's right. Ovid, whose full name was Publius Ovidius Naso, lived from 43 B.C. to 18 A.D. Ovid wrote after Virgil did, but his writing was different from Virgil's.

MEMBER #1: How was it different?

APU: If I may answer this question, Virgil wrote poems to teach people lessons. Ovid wrote simply because he believed that poetry was beautiful.

JULIO RIVERA: That's right.

MARGOT: It seems like a lot of famous Romans were banished from the city. Why was Ovid banished?

JULIO RIVERA: He was forced to leave Rome at the age of 50, but the reasons why are unclear. It seems that he offended a member of the family of the emperor Augustus. He lived his last years in a cold and unpleasant town on the Black Sea. Still, Ovid is responsible for most of what we know of Greek and Roman myths, many of which had never been written down before.

MEMBER #3: Wasn't his most famous book called, uh … *Meta*-something?

APU: *Metamorphosis.* It means "change."

JULIO RIVERA: Right. Today, I thought we would read together from an English adaptation of a myth that appears in *The Metamorphosis*. It is the story of Icarus and Daedalus, adapted from *Bulfinch's Mythology*. As Apu said, *metamorphosis* means "change." And all of these stories involve a change of some kind. In the story of Daphne and Apollo, for instance, Daphne changes from a young woman into a tree. Keep an eye out for the change in this story.

MARGOT: Please pass around these copies of the story, and we'll go in a circle to read.

[Julio Rivera hands copies to Nancy to pass out to the group. Nancy begins reading.]

NANCY: Daedalus was a skillful artist who created the labyrinth, in which the monstrous Minotaur was housed and from which Theseus escaped.

MEMBER #1: The labyrinth was a structure with countless winding passages and corners that turned into more halls and corners. It seemed to have no beginning and no end, like the river Maeander, which bends and turns in its path to the sea.

MEMBER #2: Daedalus built the labyrinth for King Minos, but afterward the king turned against him, and Daedalus was shut up in a tower.

MEMBER #3: Daedalus wanted to escape from his prison, but knew that he could not leave the island by sea because the king kept a close eye on all the ships and boats. No ship could sail without being carefully searched.

MEMBER #4: "Minos may control the land and sea," said Daedalus, "but not the sky. I will try that way." So he set to work to fashion wings for himself and his young son, Icarus.

MARGOT: He tied feathers together, beginning with the smallest and adding larger ones to expand the wings' surface. He secured the larger ones with thread and the smaller ones with wax, and shaped the set of wings with a gentle curve like the wings of a bird.

JULIO RIVERA: Icarus, the boy, stood and looked on, sometimes running to gather up the feathers the wind had blown away. Then he would play with the wax, kneading it with his fingers, and sometimes getting in the way of his father's work.

APU: When his work was done, Daedalus, waving his wings, lifted himself up and hung in place in mid-air. He came down and outfitted his son and taught him how to fly like a bird tempting her young ones out of their nest.

NANCY: When the preparations for flight were complete, he said, "Icarus, my son, I command you to keep at a moderate height, for if you fly too low, the dampness of the sea will clog your wings, and if you fly too high, the heat of the sun will melt them. Stay near me, and you will be safe."

© Harcourt

MEMBER #1:	As he gave those instructions and fitted the wings to his son's shoulders, Daedalus' face was wet with tears, and his hands trembled.
MEMBER #2:	He kissed the boy, not knowing it would be for the last time.
MEMBER #3:	Rising on his wings, he flew off and looked back from his own flight to see how his son was doing.
MEMBER #4:	As they flew, the plowman stopped his work to gaze, and the shepherd leaned on his staff and watched them. Both were astonished and thought the figures were gods.
MARGOT:	Daedalus and Icarus passed Samos and Delos on the left and Lebynthos on the right. Then Icarus, swept up in the joy of flight, began to leave the path of his father and soar upward as if to reach heaven.
JULIO RIVERA:	The nearness of the blazing sun softened the wax that held the feathers together, and they came off. He fluttered with his arms, but no feathers remained to hold the air.
APU:	While his mouth uttered cries to his father, Icarus was submerged in the blue waters of the sea.
NANCY:	His father cried, "Icarus, Icarus, where are you?"
MEMBER #1:	At last, he saw feathers floating on the water. Bitterly regretting what he had done, Daedalus buried the body and called the land Icaria in memory of his child.
MEMBER #2:	Daedalus arrived safely in Sicily, where he built a temple to Apollo and hung up his wings, an offering to the god.
JULIO RIVERA:	And that's the story.
MEMBERS:	(*applaud*)
NANCY:	Thank you for that lesson, Mr. Julio Rivera. Our next guest today will tell us about the history of the Roman calendar. Please welcome Ms. April May.

THE END

UNIT 6 Simulations and Games

TIC-TAC-TOE WITH A TWIST   This is a twist on an old classic. Divide the class into two teams. Ask each team to devise a list of ten to fifteen questions about the founding of Rome, the Roman republic, or religion in the Roman Empire. Tell students that the questions should start simply and get increasingly more difficult. Quickly review each team's questions to ensure fair play, and then draw a giant tic-tac-toe grid on the board. Flip a coin to determine which team goes first. Each team should appoint one person to read the questions as needed. A team must answer a question correctly to be able to put an *X* or *O* on the board. Each student may answer only one question until each team member has had the chance to answer a question. Play continues until one team gets 3 *Xs* or 3 *Os* in a row. *GAME*

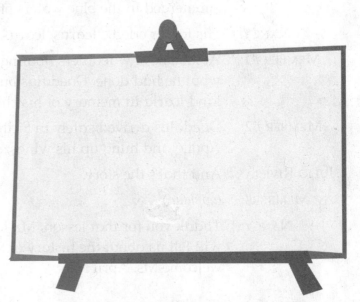

ADD A FACT!   This game will test students' knowledge of Rome and related facts. Divide students into two groups. Say a word or phrase, such as *Roman republic*, to the first group. The group must come up with one accurate fact about the Roman republic. Then the second group must add a fact about the Roman republic. Play continues until one of the groups does not have a fact to add. The point goes to the last team to give a fact. You may decide if there is a penalty for incorrect facts. Try to use words and phrases about which more than one thing may be said, such as *Italian Peninsula, Roman gods and goddesses, Roman expansion, the Punic Wars, Julius Caesar, Augustus,* and so on. The team with the most points at the end of a specified time wins. *GAME*

UNIT DRAWING GAME This popular game requires some preparation beforehand. Design a stack of about 50 cards that contain words related to the founding of Rome, the Roman republic, or religion in the Roman Empire. Obtain an hourglass or a stopwatch. Divide the class into teams of five to seven members. Have each team select one sketcher. Give a card to the first team's sketcher, and invite the student to the chalkboard. Start the timer. As the sketcher attempts to draw the word that appears on the card, the other team members must guess it in the allotted time. If they can not, give the next team a short time to figure it out. A team should receive one point each time it correctly identifies a sketch. Play proceeds in this manner until all teams have been represented. In successive rounds, each team selects a new sketcher. The game should continue until every person has had a chance to sketch. *GAME*

THE ROMAN REPUBLIC & THE AMERICAN GOVERNMENT

The Roman Republic was designed to have three parts—the consuls, the Senate, and the assemblies. In a similar fashion, our American government is made up of three branches—the legislative, the executive, and the judicial. Divide the class into two parts. One half of the class should represent the Roman Republic, and the other half should represent the American government as it exists today. Ask each side to prepare a short presentation about the basics of its governmental structure for a summit meeting with foreign powers. Ask each side to explain how its particular structure best suits the needs of the people it governs. Stage a mock summit meeting where each side makes its presentation. Students may ask each other questions about the function or design of the governments when the presentations are finished. If time allows, encourage students to use ideas from both the Roman Republic and the American government to brainstorm a new government that combines the best features of each. *SIMULATION*

UNIT 6 Long-Term Project

THE QUESTAURANT: REVIEWING ANCIENT ROME

The word *restaurant* comes from the Latin word *restaurare*, which means to restore, or build up again. In this project, students will design a restaurant where customers go to restore their minds with knowledge of Ancient Rome. The name for the place where this new kind of educational dining experience occurs is the "Questaurant."

Week 1

👥 group   🕐 45 minutes

Materials: paper, pens, resource materials

Introduce the project by explaining the idea behind the questaurant. Divide the students into four groups. Each group will create its own questaurant by designing three elements: the menu, a mural, and a tablecloth. The menu contains all of the knowledge a customer can "try" in the form of questions. Five true/false and five fill-in-the blank questions serve as "Appetizers." Ten open-ended questions serve as "Main Course" options. A separate "Dessert" menu is the answer key. The mural and tablecloth are where diners go in quest of answers. The tablecloth will contain detailed maps to help with geography questions. The mural will feature an illustrated timeline and other information to rebuild knowledge of events, dates, people, gods, and goddesses. The questions asked on the menu will determine what needs to be included in the mural and on the tablecloth. Have groups start writing questions for their menus. For next week, each student should bring in five questions and answers for his or her group.

Week 2

👥 group   🕐 45 minutes

Materials: paper, pens, tablecloth material, colored pencils and markers, resource materials

This week, students will sort through their questions and decide which they will use (about 25 in all). Students may need to change the format of some questions. They should then make a list of the answers they need to include on their tablecloths and murals. Once they've decided, they should design their maps on the tablecloths. The tablecloths should include answers to all geography-related questions. The maps should include a compass and any important natural features, such as rivers and mountain ranges.

© Harcourt

Week 3

group · **45 minutes**

Materials: mural paper, pens, yardsticks, markers or crayons, glue, staplers, resource materials

Once students have decided on their menus and have finished their tablecloths, they are now ready to start on their murals. Students should consult their list of the events, dates, people, gods, and goddesses they will need to include. They should then decide how to lay out the paper. Remind them that information is the most important concern, but appearance matters, too. Their questaurants should be attractive places to visit. One student in each group should be placed in charge of making five copies each of the main menu and the dessert menu. Menu pages should be assembled in order and stapled.

Week 4

group · **45 minutes**

Materials: pens, pencils

By this week, the preparations have been made and all the work should be complete. It's time for the grand opening of the class questaurants. Arrange the desks into four restaurant-size tables. Murals should be hung. Tablecloths should be put in place. Menus should be laid on the tables. Each group should try the items at a neighboring questaurant, recording their answers as they go. When they are finished, they should ask a questaurant "waiter" from that group for the dessert menu. If time allows, have the class discuss the project and evaluate how the different groups handled their challenges.

Tips for combination classrooms:

 For grade five, add information about the major military battles and campaigns of the Revolutionary War, and create a corresponding map.

 For grade seven, discuss the experience of Christians, Jews, and Muslims during the religious crusades in Europe, and compare it to the experience of Jews and Christians during the time of the Roman Empire.

© Harcourt

6 Short-Term Projects

These projects challenge students to depict the culture of ancient Rome using everyday models such as playbills, postcards, and posters.

Cast of Emperors
👤 individual   🕐 40 minutes

Materials: pens, paper, glue, magazines, resource materials

Invite your students to imagine that a play has been produced depicting four to six Roman emperors. Each student works for *Playcard*, a program handed out at Broadway shows. Their task is to create a two-page spread. Laid out side-by-side, each page will feature a photo and short biography for each emperor. Students may decide which two emperors to portray. For example, they might choose one "good" emperor and one "bad" emperor. An emperor's image can be the actual emperor, or a modern actor who would play that emperor well. Students can search for images in magazines or on the Internet. Images should be marked with the emperor's name and dates of rule. Short biographical paragraphs should briefly tell of events in each emperor's life, ranging from major feats to failures and death.

Roman Holiday
👤 individual   🕐 30 minutes

Materials: blank postcards, pens, colored pencils or markers, resource materials

Tourists to foreign cities often flock to the most popular architectural sites and monuments. Rome has many of these to offer. Have students create a postcard of the Aqueduct of Claudius, the Arch of Constantine, the Temple of Jupiter, the Colosseum, or the Pantheon. They will draw the site on one side. On the other side, they will write a brief note to a friend, identifying the place and telling of its history and significance.

© Harcourt

Bread and Circus

🧍🧍🧍 small group   🕐 30 minutes

Materials: posterboard, colored pencils or markers, resource materials

Will it be a chariot race, footrace, boxing, wrestling, or javelin throwing? Or will it be a gladiator show? Divide the students into small groups and have each group decide which ancient Roman event they would like to advertise. Then they will create a poster to attract as many people as possible to the event. Remind students that posters should include the name of the place and the date when the event will take place.

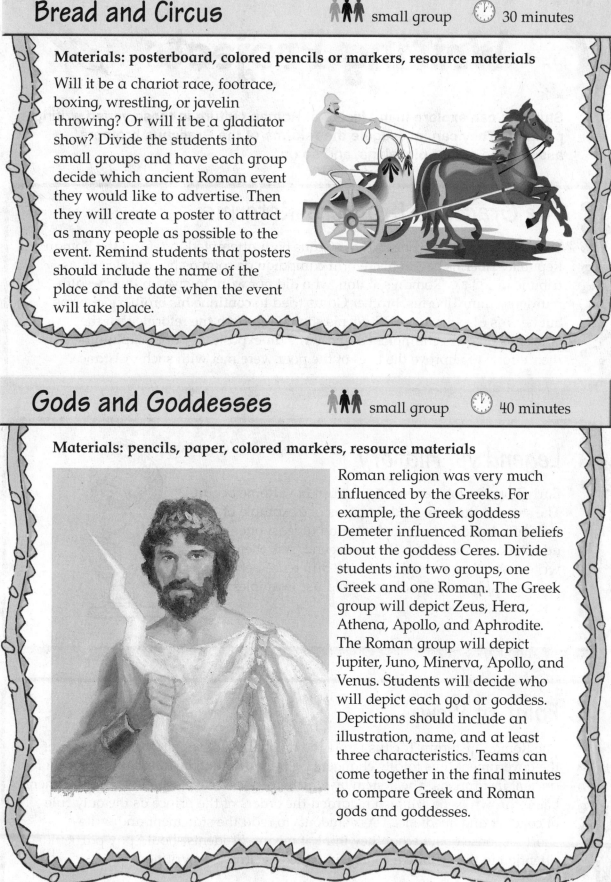

Gods and Goddesses

🧍🧍🧍 small group   🕐 40 minutes

Materials: pencils, paper, colored markers, resource materials

Roman religion was very much influenced by the Greeks. For example, the Greek goddess Demeter influenced Roman beliefs about the goddess Ceres. Divide students into two groups, one Greek and one Roman. The Greek group will depict Zeus, Hera, Athena, Apollo, and Aphrodite. The Roman group will depict Jupiter, Juno, Minerva, Apollo, and Venus. Students will decide who will depict each god or goddess. Depictions should include an illustration, name, and at least three characteristics. Teams can come together in the final minutes to compare Greek and Roman gods and goddesses.

Writing Projects

Students can explore many facets of Roman culture in these varied writing prompts. They can investigate the reforms of the Gracchus brothers, assume the role of plebeians, and so on.

The Gracchus Brothers' Reforms

Tiberius Gracchus and his brother Gaius both attempted to reform the Roman Republic. Tiberius began his reform campaign as soon as he was elected as tribune in 133 B.C. Roman senators who did not want to give up their wealth murdered him. Tiberius' brother Gaius tried to continue his brother's reforms, but he was also murdered. Students should research the reforms that the Gracchus brothers championed and write an expository paper explaining why their efforts to improve the lives of the poor were met with such resistance.

Legend vs. History

Early Romans told legends to explain how Rome began. The story of Romulus and Remus is one example of a Roman legend. Have students find at least one additional example of a Roman legend. Ask them to write a short paper explaining the difference between legend and history. Students should use examples of each in their writing.

Point of View

The Roman historian Tacitus wrote the following statement: "The character of the government thus totally changed; no traces were to be found of the spirit of ancient institutions. The system by which every citizen shared in the government being thrown aside, all men regarded the orders of the prince as the only rule of conduct and obedience." Ask students to read the statement and write a short response about what they think it means. Students should pay particular attention to the historical context in which Tacitus was writing.

A Plebeian Life

There were two social classes in the Roman Republic—the patricians and the plebeians. The patrician class had wealth, social standing, and was the only group of citizens that could become senators. The plebeians were everyone else except for slaves and foreigners. The plebeians had difficult lives. They were forced to leave their homes to defend Rome, but when they returned, they often found that their homes had been destroyed in the conflict. Finally, the plebeians decided to do something about their situation. Ask students to take the role of a plebeian citizen and write a letter to other plebeians asking for their support in the refusal to fight in the Roman army. Students should try to capture the emotion of the time. For example, a letter could be written by a plebeian who has just found his home destroyed. Students should also consider the magnitude of what the letters they are writing propose—the poor class taking a stand against the wealthy and powerful class of patricians.

Magazine Feature

The lives of rich Romans and poor Romans were radically different in the Roman Empire. Ask students to write a magazine article that compares and contrasts the lives of the rich and the poor. Students should write as if they were living in ancient Roman times and include imaginary quotes from both rich and poor Romans in their articles. Students should strive to accurately represent the daily lives of each class of Roman citizen.

Roman Religions

Because of its size and the variety of cultures living in the Roman Empire, many different religions were practiced by the people of the Roman Empire. Ask students to write an essay in which they explore the different religions of the Roman Empire. What were some of the religions that people practiced? What part did religion play in Roman society? How was the government involved with the practice of religion? What problems arose because of differences in religions? Students should attempt to answer these questions in essay form. Remind students to support their answers with examples.

Daily Geography

1. **Place** — On which kind of landform is Italy located?

2. **Place** — Which three bodies of water surround the Italian Peninsula?

3. **Place** — Which mountain range runs through most of the Italian Peninsula?

4. **Place** — At one time, some of the mountains in the Apennines made up which kind of landform?

5. **Human-Environment Interactions** — What are two factors that make the land on the Italian Peninsula good for farming?

6. **Movement** — The people who became known as the Latins began migrating to the Italian Peninsula around 1000 B.C. From where did these people come?

7. **Human-Environment Interactions** — Where on the Italian Peninsula did the Latins choose to settle?

8. **Location** — On which river in central Italy is the city of Rome located?

9. **Human-Environment Interactions** — By 272 B.C., Rome had gained control of the Italian Peninsula. What enemies did they have to conquer from the north, south, and east?

10. **Movement** — Which path did Carthaginian general Hannibal take in his attack on Rome?

11. **Place** — Which mountain range stretches across northern Italy?

12. **Movement** — Where did the Roman general Scipio march with his troops to save Rome and defeat Hannibal?

13. **Location** — Where was Carthage located?

14. **Place** — In 146 B.C., the Roman general Mummius conquered an important city in Greece and made it a new Roman province. What was the Greek city?

© Harcourt

15. Place   Which small kingdom did King Attalus III peacefully turn over to Rome just before he died?

16. Place   Which body of water became known as the "Roman Lake" because Rome controlled nearly all the lands surrounding it?

17. Place   Which present-day country was known as Gaul at the time of the Roman Empire?

18. Movement   Caesar made his intentions to rule Rome clear when he crossed which river between Gaul and the Italian Peninsula?

19. Location   In 37 B.C., what was the only land on the Mediterranean not under Roman control?

20. Regions   Under Augustus, the Roman Empire spread across which continents?

21. Human-Environment Interactions   What did the Romans build that helped link the empire together and made it easier to expand?

22. Place   What disaster struck Rome in A.D. 64?

23. Location   When Titus destroyed Jerusalem in A.D. 70, in what Roman province was it located?

24. Human-Environment Interactions   What kind of structures did Roman leaders build to move water from natural sources into the towns?

25. Place   What was the name of the building in ancient Rome where sports events were held?

26. Place   What was the name of the largest arena in Rome where gladiator shows were held?

27. Human-Environment Interactions   What did the Romans build so that Roman priests could make offerings and sacrifices to the gods?

28. Regions   In A.D. 115, Jews from which regions rebelled against the Romans?

29. Regions   After the Jewish rebellion in A.D. 132, Roman emperor Hadrian forbade Jews to enter Jerusalem and changed the name of Judaea to what?

30. Location   Experts believe that Jesus was born in 4 B.C. In which town in Judaea was he born?

Why Character Counts

- Respect
- Fairness
- Responsibility
- Patriotism
- Caring
- **Trustworthiness**

Trustworthiness

Trustworthiness—the word is a mouthful, but its meaning is simple. It means "worthy" or "deserving of trust." Can you think of someone you really trust? We know when someone has broken our trust, but finding someone whom we consider trustworthy can be more complicated. Being trustworthy is a big responsibility. We expect trustworthy people to be reliable and dependable.

Rome had its share of trustworthy and untrustworthy leaders. Tarquinius Superbus is a good example of an untrustworthy king. He ignored the law and stole from the people. Augustus, on the other hand, was a trustworthy leader. He ruled the Roman Empire for more than 40 years.

In your own words:

Write a definition for the word *trustworthiness*.

_____

_____

_____

© Harcourt

Name ______________________________

Character Activity

Think about the character trait of trustworthiness. What do you think is the most important reason to be trustworthy? What happens when people are not trustworthy? Is it possible to trust someone again once he or she has broken your trust? Write a short essay in which you answer these questions. Support your opinions with examples.

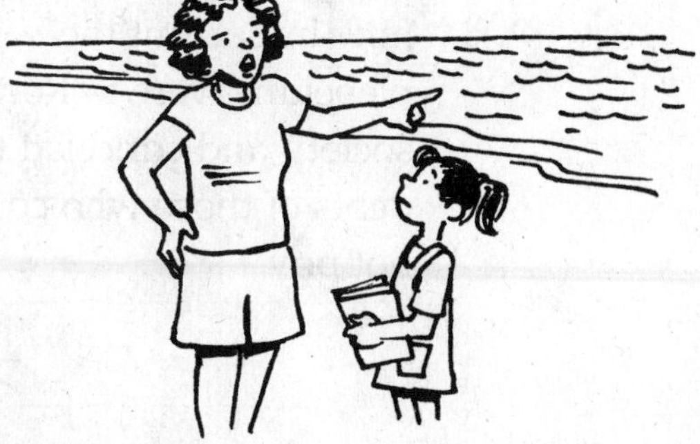

6 Economic Literacy

Credit

Have you ever borrowed money from your parents so you could buy something? Did you promise to pay the money back? If you did, you used a form of credit. Credit is widely used as a way to pay for consumer goods. Credit is a form of payment that is like a promise. When you use credit, you buy something now and promise to pay for it later. If you cannot pay back all the money, you are in debt. Debt is the money that you owe to a company or person.

Many Americans use credit cards to make purchases. Credit cards are not bad to have, but they can be easily abused. It can be hard to exercise self-control when making purchases with credit cards. In most cases, if you buy something using a credit card, you should be able to pay off the money you owe within a month. If you are not able to pay the full balance, the credit card company will charge you a fee for the money you still owe. Many people have found themselves in debt because they cannot pay off the money that they owe each month.

In ancient Rome, the plebeians used a form of credit, but it was much different than the credit cards we use today. Plebeians often had to leave their homes to fight in the Roman army. When they returned, they sometimes found that enemies had destroyed their homes and land. In order to start rebuilding their lives again, the plebeians had to borrow money from the patricians. If the plebeians were unable to pay their debts, however, they could be put in prison or used as slaves. Eventually, the plebeians led a peaceful resistance and refused to fight for Rome. The patricians realized how important the plebeians were to Roman society and canceled the debts of those who could not pay.

Credit Activity

Recall what you know about credit. Not including credit cards, what other kinds of credit are there? Are there some things that people must use credit to buy? What are they?

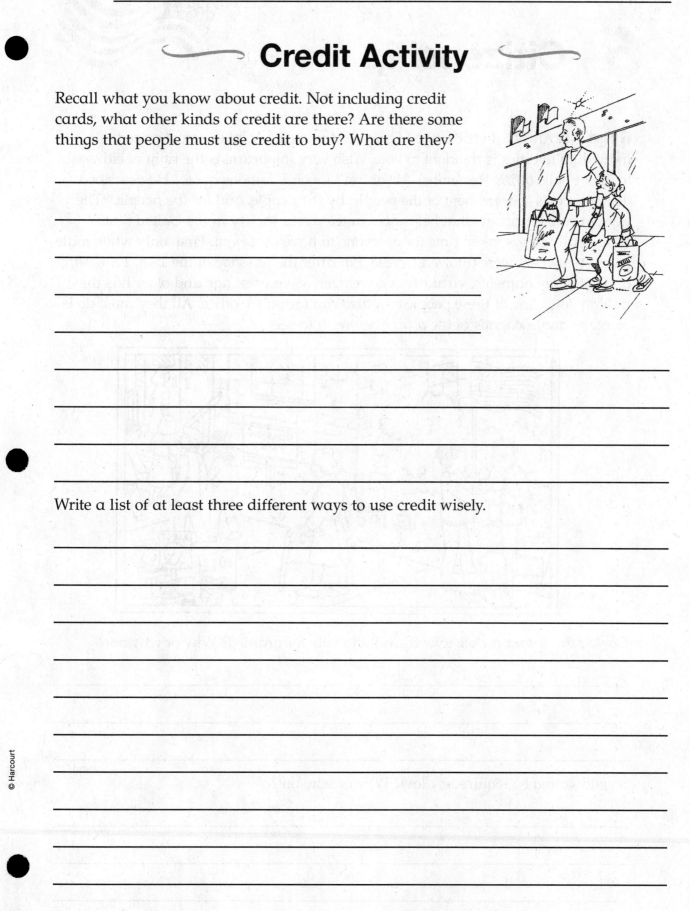

_____

_____

_____

_____

_____

_____

Write a list of at least three different ways to use credit wisely.

_____

_____

_____

_____

_____

_____

_____

UNIT
6 Citizenship

Read About It   In the United States of America, one of the most prized individual liberties is the right to vote. Also very important is the right of citizens to seek public office. Remember Abraham Lincoln's famous quote? He described democracy as "government of the people, by the people, and for the people." The right to vote is part of what helps guarantee a free society in the United States. Historically, it has taken time for everyone to have that right. First, only white male property owners were allowed to vote. But after the passage of the 15th, 19th, 24th, and 26th Amendments, virtually every citizen 18 years of age and older has the right to vote. Any of these people can also run for public office. All they must do is meet the qualifications of the office they wish to seek.

Do you think that people take the right to vote for granted? Why or why not?

_____

_____

_____

Should voting be required by law? Why or why not?

_____

_____

_____

© Harcourt

Name _____

Talk About It Voting has become easier than ever before. You can cast your ballot early if you will be out of town for the election. In some states, you can even register to vote on Election Day. In other states, you may be allowed to mail in your vote. So, why aren't more people voting? According to one source, more than 69% of eligible voters went to the polls in the presidential election of 1964. In the year 2000, less than 50% of eligible voters voted. What are some possible reasons that people don't vote?

Write About It In the early days of the Roman Republic, the assemblies were made up of all adult male citizens of Rome. By electing new consuls each year, the new government in Rome attempted to limit the power of the consuls. How did this system work? Was it successful? Write a short essay in which you answer these questions. Think carefully about your response, and support your essay with examples.

_____

_____

_____

_____

_____

_____

_____

_____

_____

_____

_____

_____

Social Studies Journal

The single most important thing I learned was . . .

Something that confused me or that I did not understand was . . .

What surprised me the most was . . .

I would like to know more about . . .

Sources I can use to find answers to my questions . . .

The part that made the greatest impact on me was . . .

© Harcourt

Reading Guide

Questions I have before reading				New questions I have after reading
Question **1**	Question **2**	Question **3**	Question **4**	Question: Question:

Summary of what I learned after reading that answers my questions				Other interesting information I learned while reading
Question **1**	Question **2**	Question **3**	Question **4**	
General summary:				My reaction to what I read:

Current Events

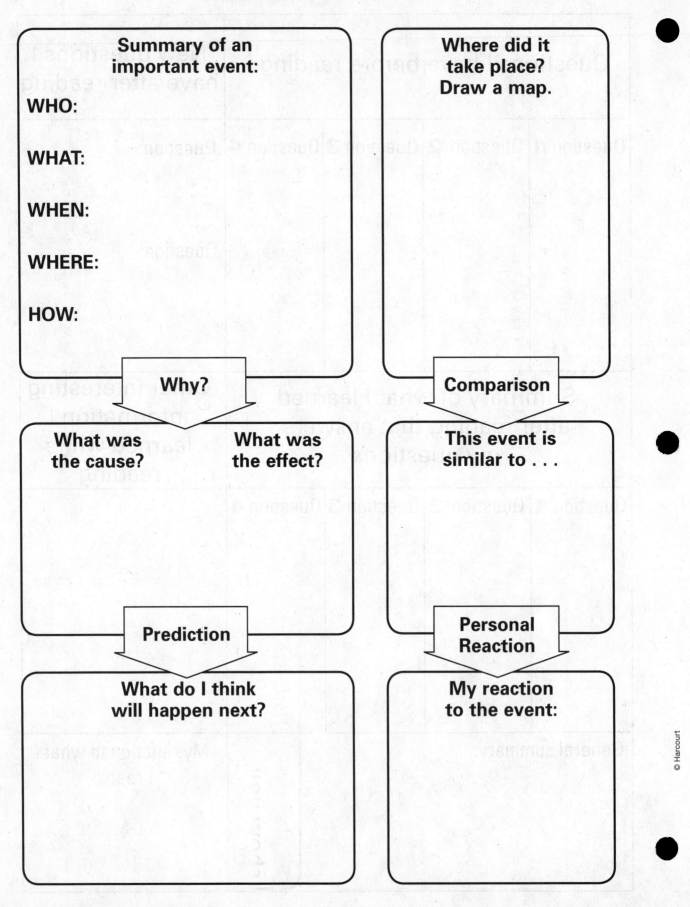

Summary of an important event:

WHO:

WHAT:

WHEN:

WHERE:

HOW:

Where did it take place? Draw a map.

Why?

What was the cause?

What was the effect?

Comparison

This event is similar to . . .

Prediction

What do I think will happen next?

Personal Reaction

My reaction to the event:

© Harcourt

Visual Literacy

Explain what is happening in the artwork.

Explain the mood of the artwork.

Describe the artwork.

Explain what the artist is trying to show you.

Main Idea and Supporting Details

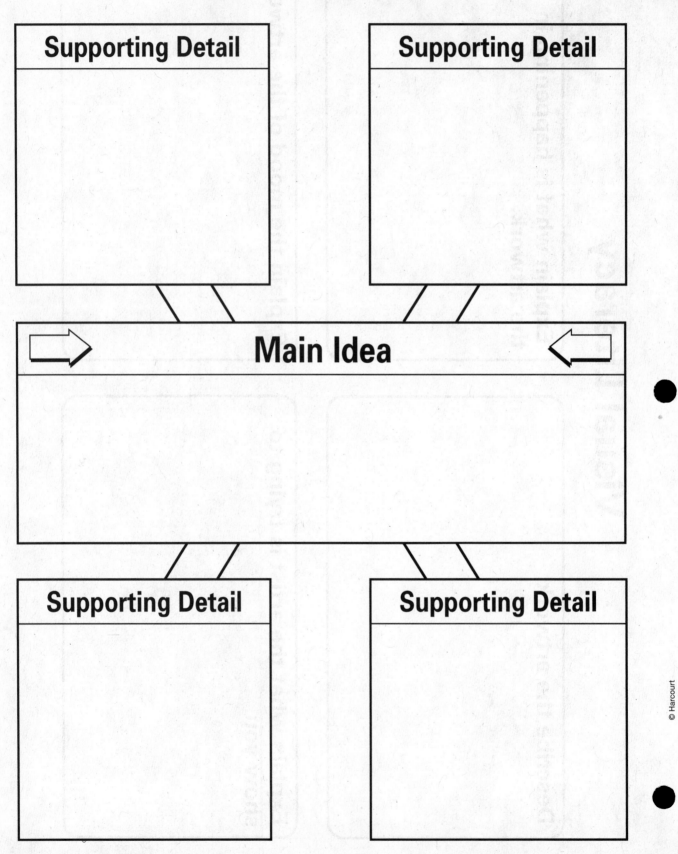

Supporting Detail

Supporting Detail

Main Idea

Supporting Detail

Supporting Detail

Fact and Opinion

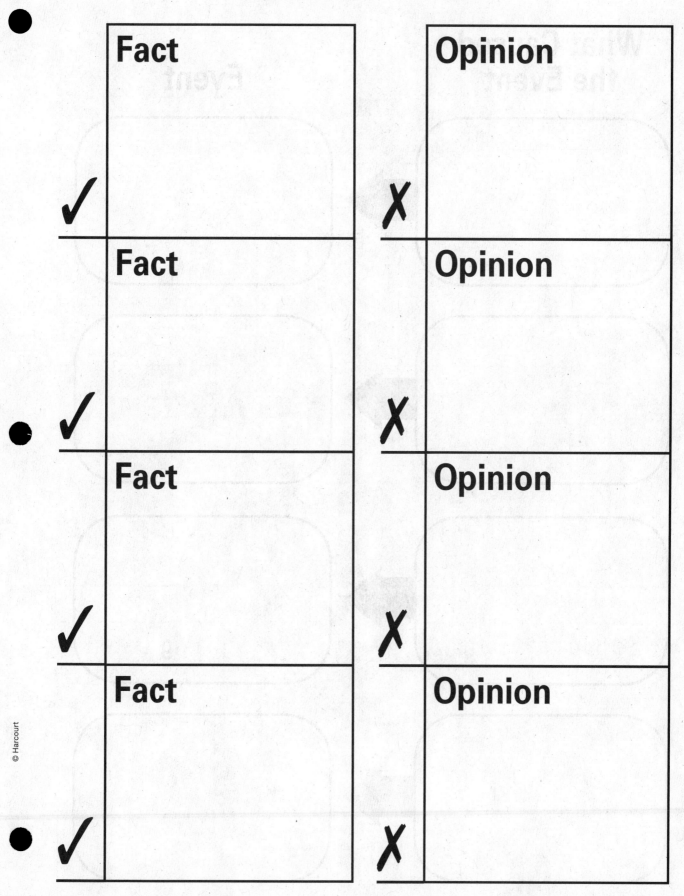

Fact	Opinion
Fact	Opinion
Fact	Opinion
Fact	Opinion

Causes and Effects

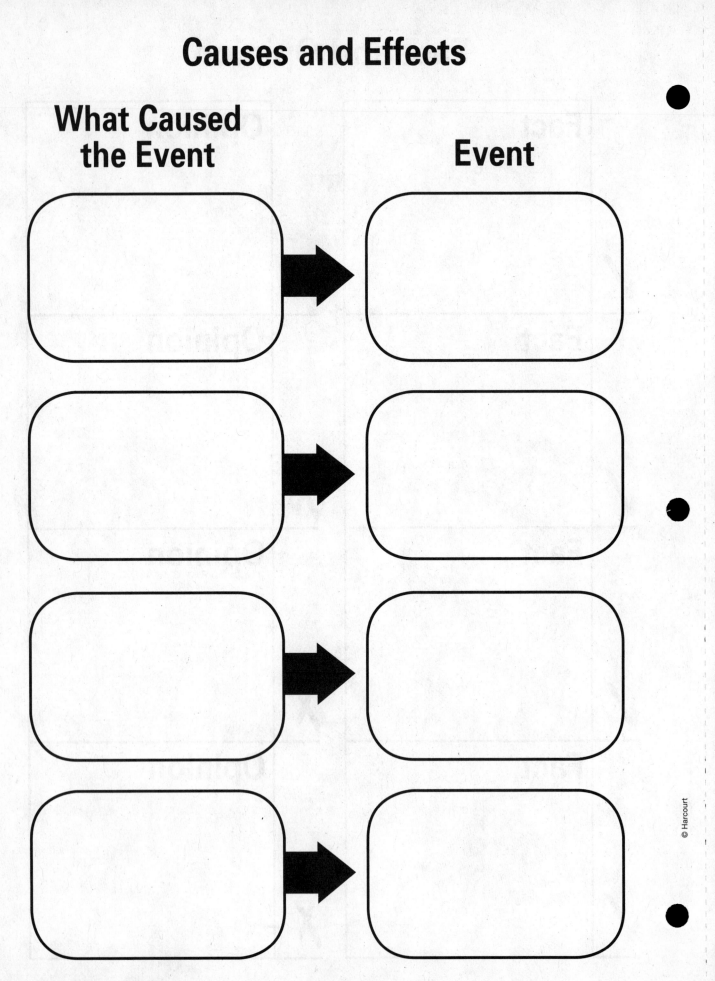

What Caused the Event

Event

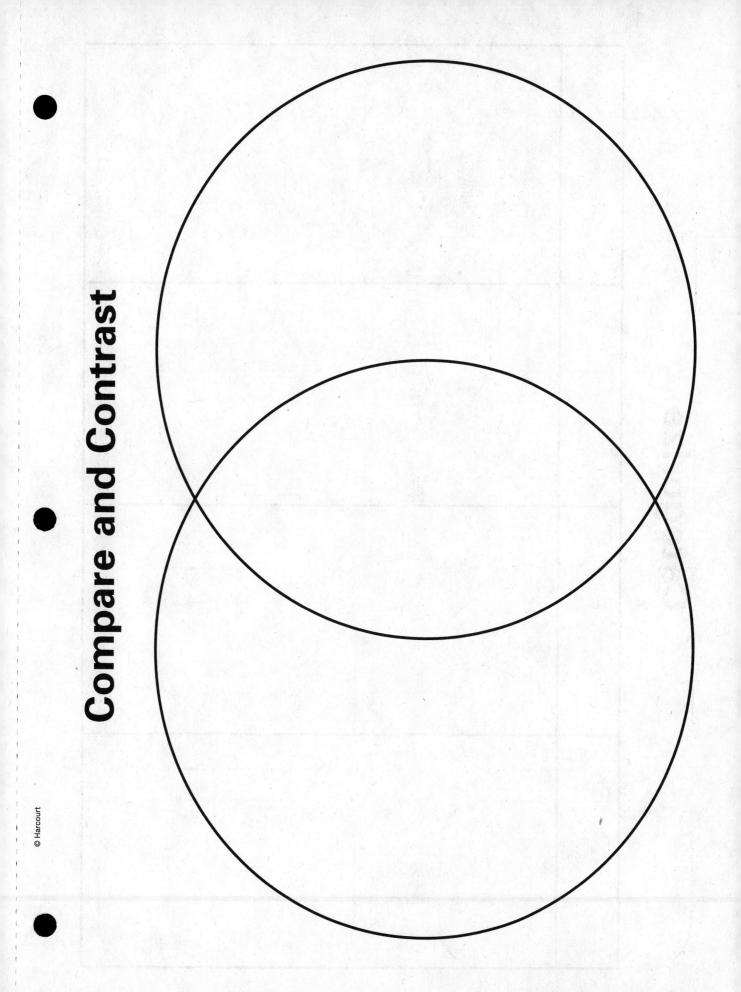

Categorize

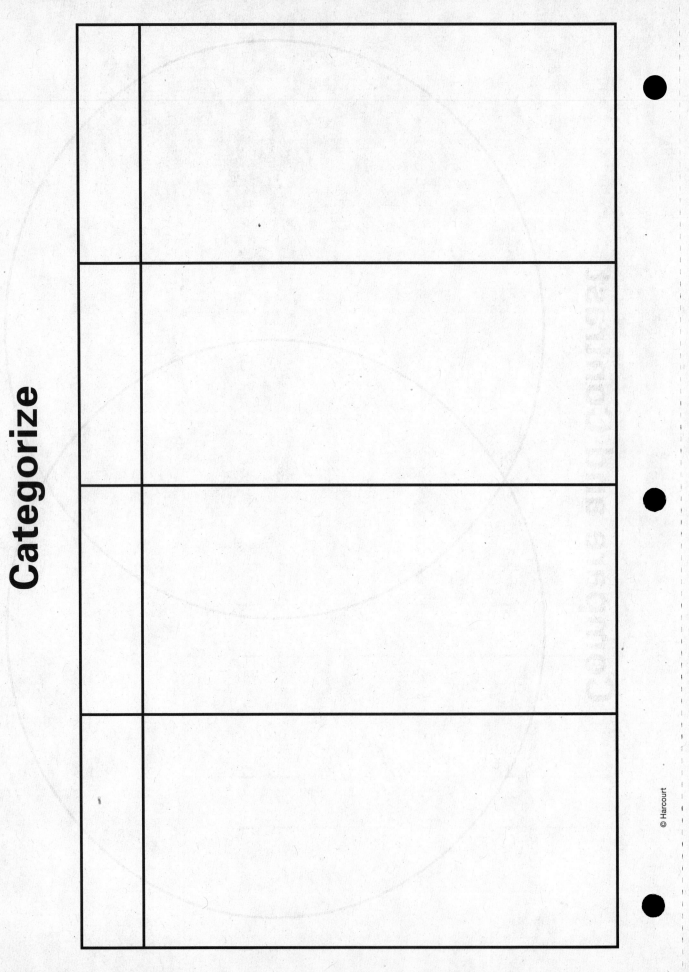

Sequence

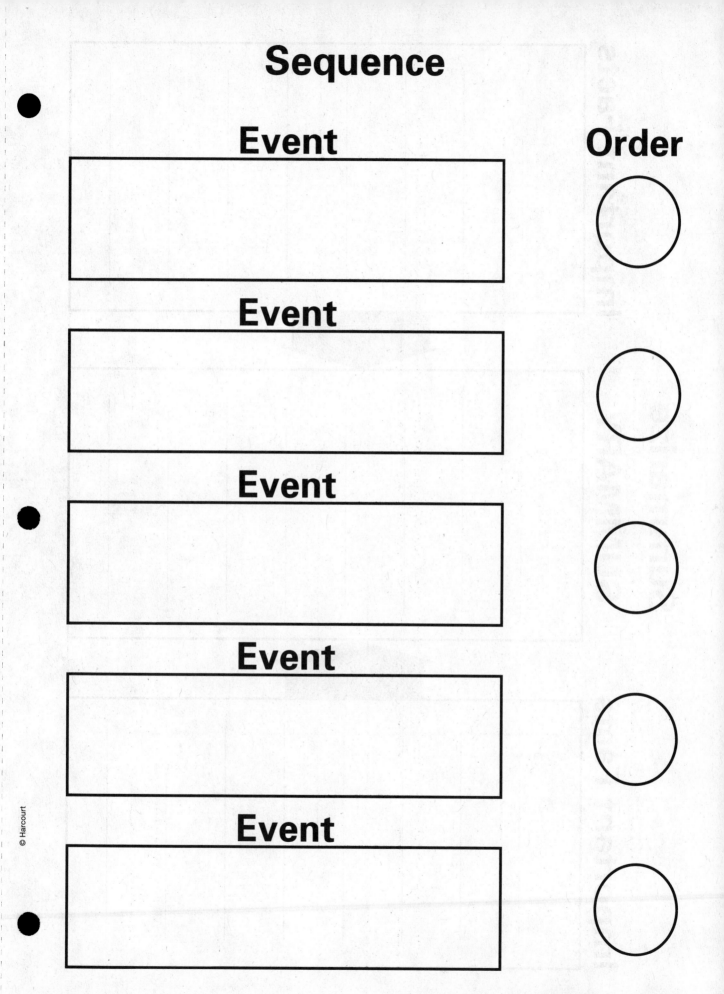

Event

Order

Event

Event

Event

Event

Summarize

Important Facts

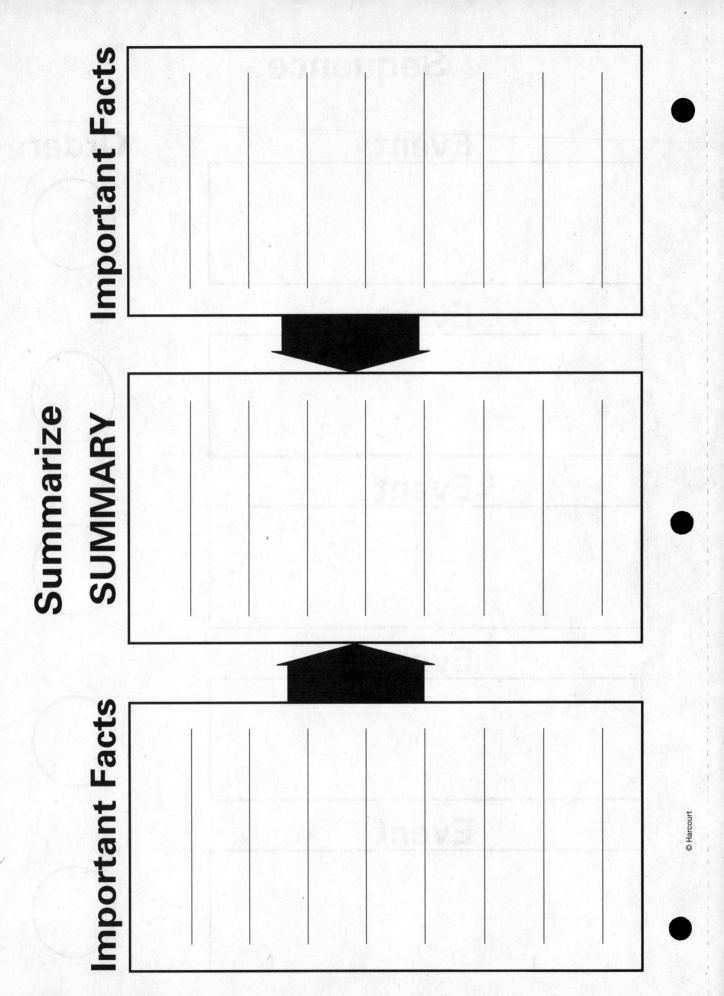

SUMMARY

Important Facts

Make a Generalization

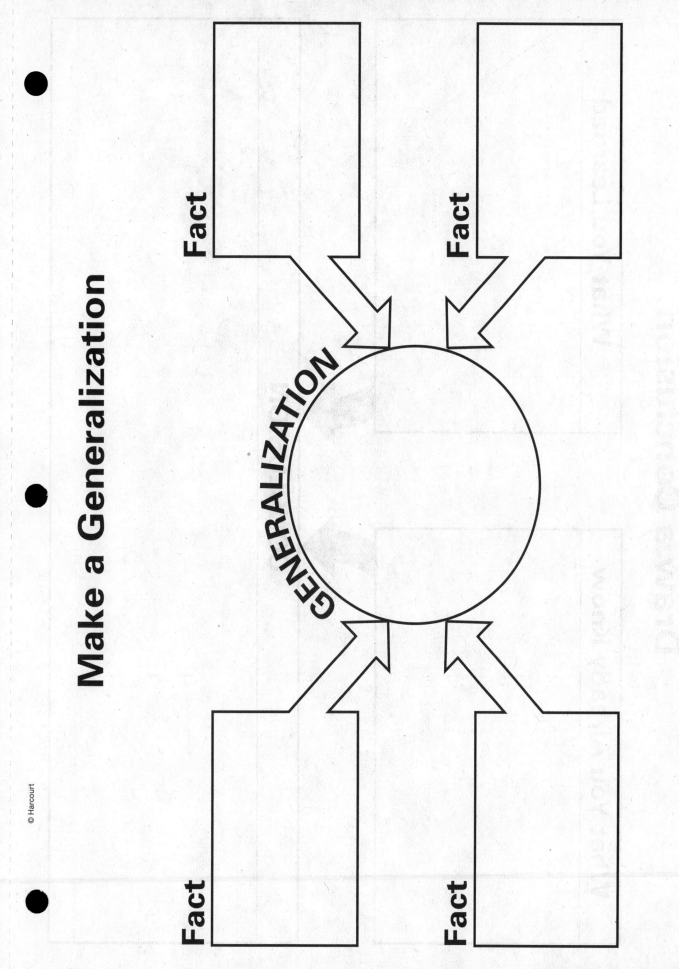

Fact

Fact

GENERALIZATION

Fact

Fact

Draw a Conclusion

What You Learned

What You Already Know

CONCLUSION

Point of View

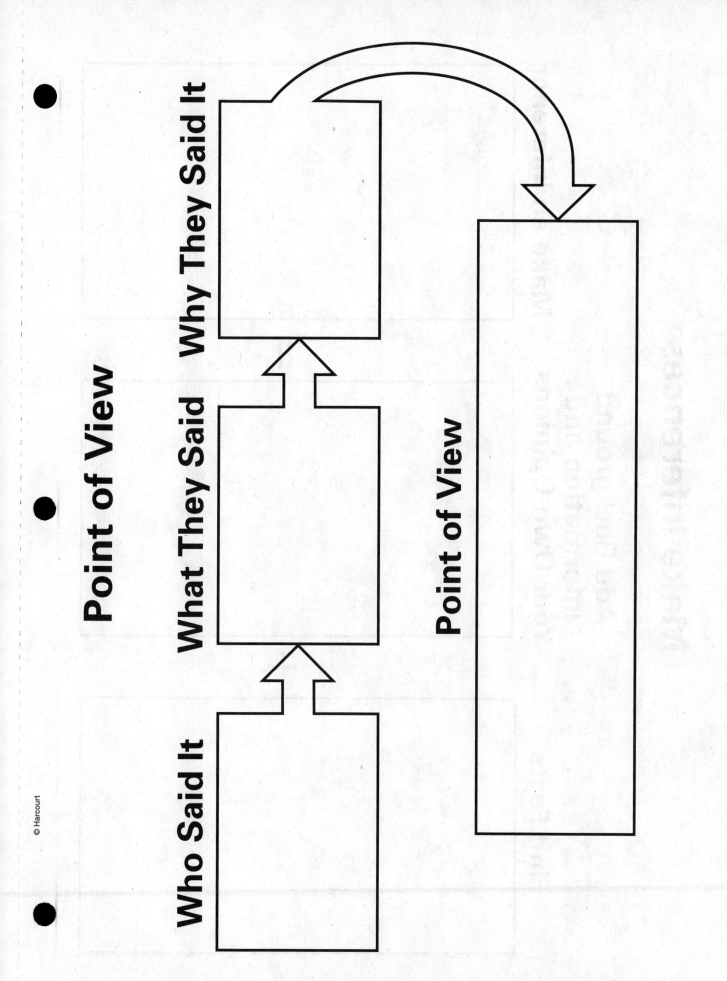

Who Said It

What They Said

Why They Said It

Point of View

Make Inferences

Make an Inference

Add Background Information and Your Own Opinions

Find Facts

=

+

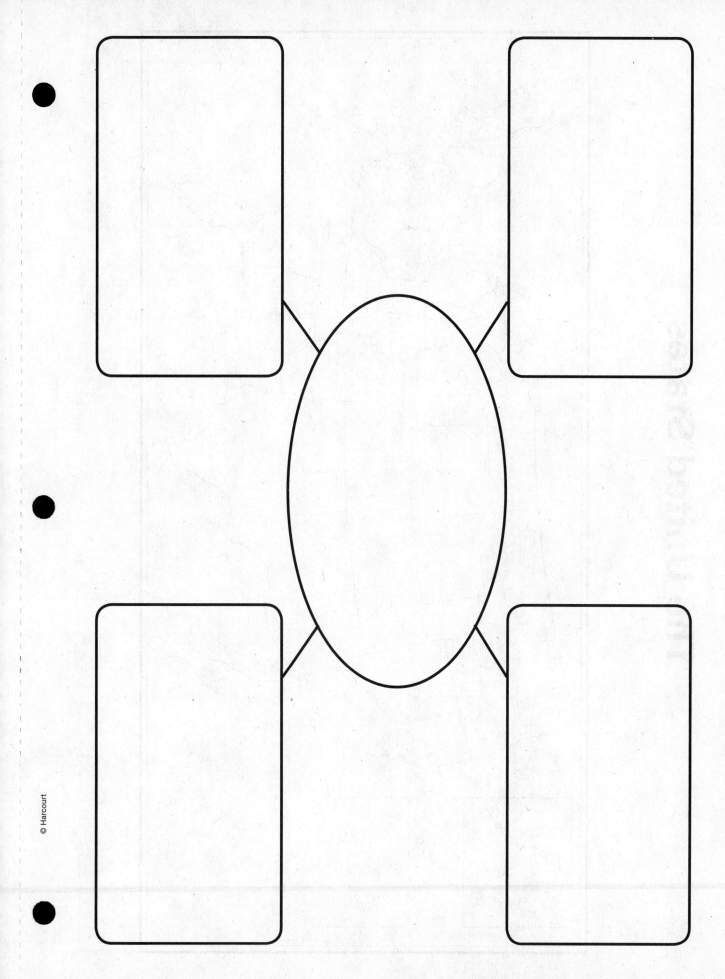

The United States

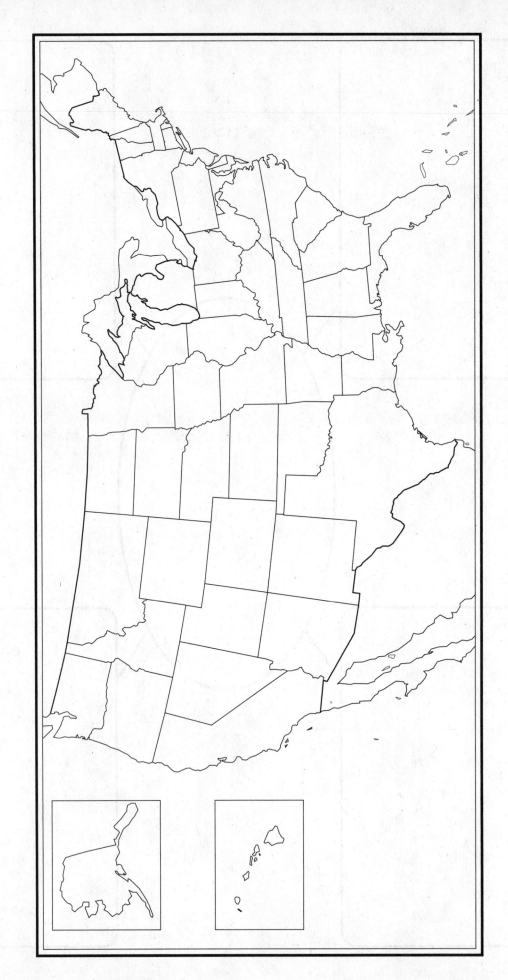

North America

The World

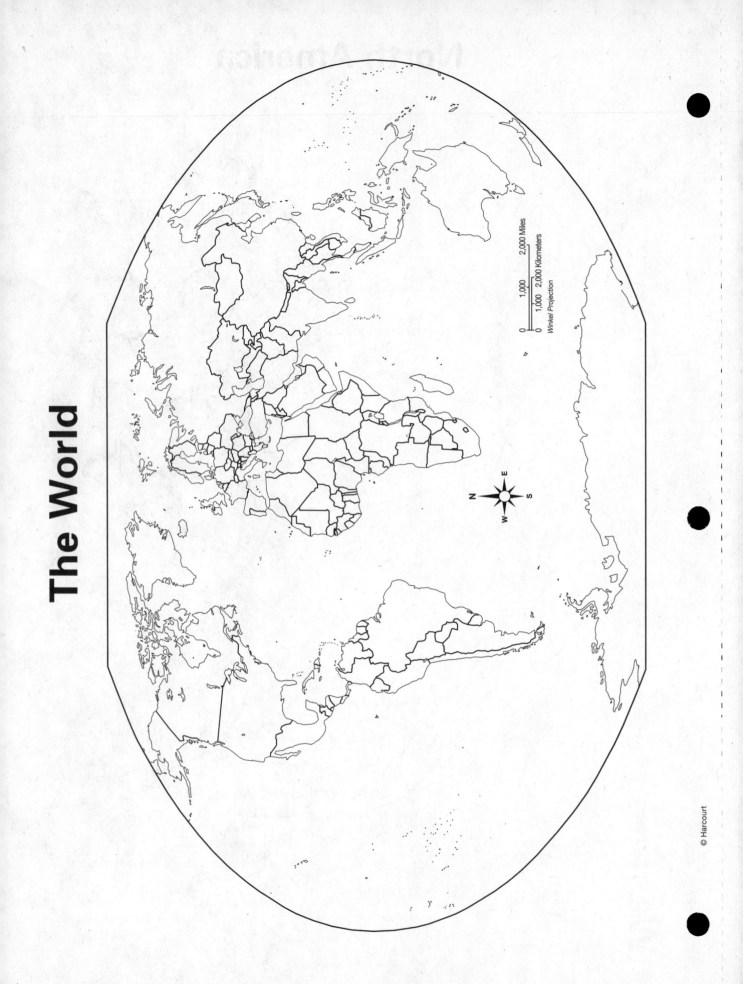

2,000 Miles

2,000 Kilometers

1,000

1,000

0

Winkel Projection

N
E
W
S

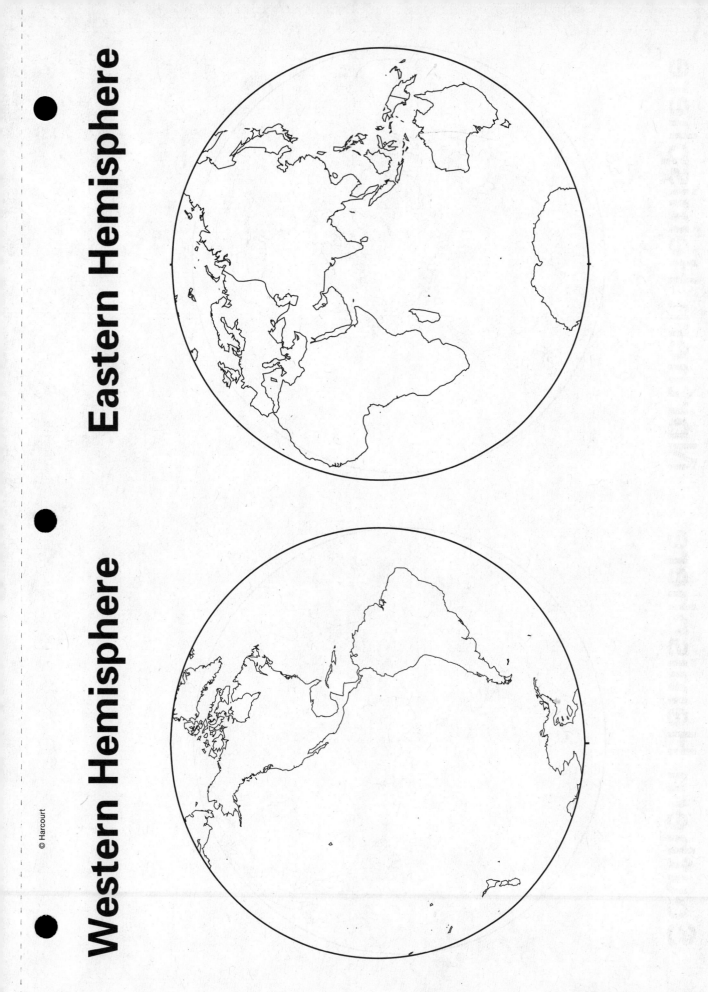

Eastern Hemisphere

Western Hemisphere

Northern Hemisphere

Southern Hemisphere

California

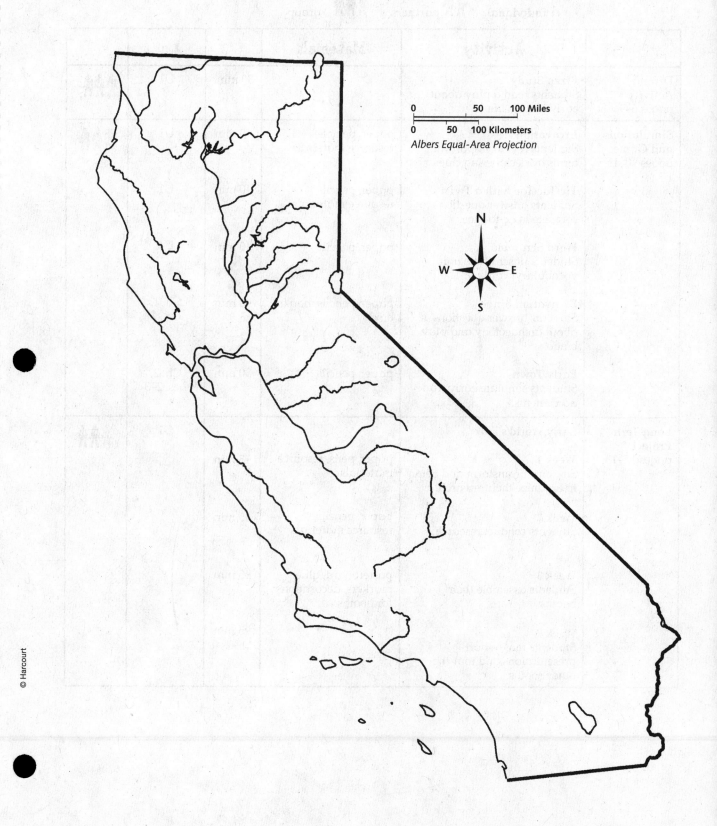

0   50   100 Miles

0   50   100 Kilometers

Albers Equal-Area Projection

N
W   E
S

UNIT 1 Planning Options

👤 individual 👥 partners 👥👤 group

	Activity	Materials	🕐	Link	
Drama Activity pages 6–9	**Pizza Study** Students read a play about early human life.		30 min.	U1	👥👤
Simulations and Games pages 10–11	**Excavation** Students review important terms by deciphering clues.	paper, pencils, resource materials	40 min	U1	👥👤
	Tic-Tac-Toe with a Twist Students answer questions to compete in tic-tac-toe.	paper, pencils, resource materials	40 min	U1	
	Word Scramble Students unscramble unit vocabulary words.	paper, pencils	40 min	U1	
	Excavation Bingo Students answer questions about archaeology and play bingo.	paper, pencils, bag or box	40 min	Ch. 1, Les. 1	
	Early Towns Students simulate early trade agreements.	paper, pencils	30 min	Ch. 2, Les. 2–3	
Long-Term Project pages 12–13	**Early World's Fair** **Week 1** Students brainstorm and begin to organize their research.	paper, pens, resource materials	45 min	U1	👥👤
	Week 2 Students conduct research.	paper, pencils, resource materials	45 min		
	Week 3 Students assemble their booths.	posterboard, glue, markers, decorations for booths	45 min		
	Week 4 Students make short presentations and tour the other booths.		45 min		

© Harcourt

	Activity	Materials	🕐	Link	
Short-Term Projects pages 14–15	**Assembling the Past** Students try to reassemble clay pots.	paint or markers, 4-5 clay pots in two different sizes, paper grocery bag, hammer, glue	40 min.	Ch. 1, Les. 1	👤👤👤
	Make a Cave Painting Students make an "ancient" painting.	brown paper grocery bag, tempera paints, paintbrushes	30 min.	Ch. 1, Les. 2	👤
	Talking History Students construct the history of an object, using clues.	classroom "artifacts"	20 min.	Ch. 1, Les. 1	👤👤
	Specialized Labor Students make replicas of ancient products.	modeling clay or colored pencils and paper	30 min.	Ch. 2, Les. 3	👤👤👤
Writing Projects pages 16–17	**Rules for the People**	paper, pencils	40 min.	Ch. 2, Les. 2–3	👤
	Family Migration	paper, pencils	30 min.	Ch. 1, Les. 2	
	The Legend of the Bison	paper, pencils	40 min.	Ch. 2, Les. 3	
	Trade Brochure	paper, colored pencils or markers	40 min.	Ch. 2, Les. 2-3	
	Breaking News	paper, pencils	40 min.	Ch. 1, Les. 1	
	Breaking the Ice Age	paper, pencils	40 min.	Ch. 1, Les.2	
Why Character Counts pages 20–21	**Respect** Students read about respect and complete the follow-up activity.	pencils	30 min.	Ch. 1, Les.2 Ch. 2, Les. 3	👤
Economic Literacy pages 22–23	**Surplus** Students read about the concept of surplus and complete the follow-up activity.	pencils	30 min.	Ch. 2, Les. 1	👤
Citizenship pages 24–25	**Government** Students read about government, hold a discussion, and complete a writing activity.	pencils	40 min.	U1	👤 👤👤👤

UNIT 2

Planning Options

♟ individual   ♟♟ partners   ♟♟♟ group

	Activity	Materials	🕐	Link	
Drama Activity pages 28–31	**Interpreting Hammurabi's Code** Students read a play about Hammurabi's Code.		30 min.	Ch. 3, Les. 5	♟♟♟
Simulations and Games pages 32–33	**Make Your Own Word Search** Students create a word search game.	graph paper, pencils	40 min.	U2	♟♟♟
	Who Rules the Spelling Dynasty? Students review vocabulary and spelling skills.		40 min.	U2	
	Add a Fact! Students compete to see who knows the most about various topics.		40 min.	U2	
	Forms of Leadership Students conduct a debate.		30 min.	Ch. 3, Les. 2	
Long-Term Project pages 34–35	**Egyptian Art Exhibition** **Week 1** Students brainstorm and begin to make a list of needed materials.	paper, pencils, resource materials	45 min.	Ch. 4, Les. 1–4	♟♟♟
	Week 2 Students conduct research.	paper, pencils, resource materials	45 min.		
	Week 3 Students create their artwork.	art materials	45 min.		
	Week 4 Students finish their artwork and make short presentations.	art materials	45 min.		

© Harcourt

	Activity	Materials	🕐	Link	
Short-Term Projects pages 36–37	**Building Pyramids** Students build pyramids.	cardboard, pencils, rulers, tape, scissors, paint, paintbrushes	40 min.	Ch. 4, Les. 2	
	Fertile Crescent Rest Stop Students design flyers and brochures.	unlined paper, colored pencils or markers	20 min.	Ch. 3, Les. 2	
	Making Cuneiform Tablets Students make clay tablets.	clay, craft sticks, resource materials	30 min.	Ch. 3, Les. 3	
	Systems of Writing Students compare cuneiform to hieroglyphs.	resource materials	30 min.	Ch. 3, Les. 3; Ch. 4 Les. 2	
	What's for Dinner? Students research the diet of ancient Egyptians.	paper, pencils, resource materials	40 min.	Ch. 4	
Writing Projects pages 38–39	**My Favorite Things**	paper, pencils	30 min.	Ch. 4, Les. 2	
	Egyptian Art	paper, pencils	40 min.	Ch. 4, Les. 4	
	The Secrets of the Rosetta Stone	paper, pencils	40 min.	Ch. 4, Les. 2	
	Write Your Own Hieroglyphs	paper, pencils	40 min.	Ch. 4, Les. 2	
	Letter of Protest	paper, pencils	40 min.	Ch. 5, Les. 1	
	River Valley Poem	paper, pencils	40 min.	Ch. 3, Les. 1	
Why Character Counts pages 42–43	**Fairness** Students read about fairness and complete the follow-up activity.	pencils	30 min.	Ch. 3, Les. 5	
Economic Literacy pages 44–45	**Cost-Benefit Analysis** Students read about the concept of the cost-benefit analysis and complete the follow-up activity.	pencils	30 min.	Ch. 4, Les. 3	
Citizenship pages 46–47	**Legislature** Students read about the United States legislature, hold a discussion, and complete a writing activity.	pencils	40 min.	Ch. 3, Les. 2	

Planning Options

👤 individual 👥 partners 👥👥 group

	Activity	Materials	🕐	Link	
Drama Activity pages 50–53	**Ancient Hebrew Hall of Fame** Students read about important characters in ancient Hebrew history.		30 min.	U3	👥👥👥
Simulations and Games pages 54–55	**Tic-Tac-Toe with a Twist** Students answer questions to compete in tic-tac-toe.	paper, pencils, resource materials	40 min.	U3	👥👥👥
	Who Am I? Students guess characters using clues.	paper, pencils, resource materials	40 min.	U3	
	Fill In the Blanks Students guess missing letters to make words.		40 min.	U3	
	Help! I'm Stranded! Students guess geographical locations using clues.	resource materials	40 min.	U3	
Long-Term Project pages 56–57	**Hebrew People—A Story in Pictures**			U3	👥👥👥
	Week 1 Students brainstorm images and artifacts to use in their projects.	paper, pencils, resource materials	30 min.		
	Week 2 Students sort through images for their montages.	paper, pencils, resource materials	45 min.		
	Week 3 Students create their montages.	images, posterboard, scissors, glue, markers	45 min.		
	Week 4 Students make a short presentation and display their artwork.	completed montages	45 min.		

© Harcourt

	Activity	Materials	🕐	Link	
Short-Term Projects pages 58–59	**Temple Layout** Students draw diagrams of King Solomon's temple.	unlined paper, colored pencils or markers, resource materials	30 min.	Ch. 6, Les. 2	
	Messages in Hebrew Students write using the Hebrew alphabet.	paper, pens, pencils or crayons, resource materials	30 min.	U3	
	The Passover Seder Students research the meaning of the Seder meal.	resource materials, markers, posterboard	30 min.	Ch 6, Les. 1	
	Compare Maps Students compare maps of Israel.	resource materials, pencils, paper	40 min.	Ch. 6, Les. 2	
Writing Projects pages 60–61	**Songs of Exodus**	paper, pencils	40 min.	Ch. 6, Les. 1	
	Solomon's Proverbs	paper, pencils	40 min.	Ch. 6, Les. 2	
	Geography and Conflict	paper, pencils	40 min.	U3	
	Cyrus's Plan	paper, pencils	30 min.	Ch. 7, Les. 1	
	A King's Biography	paper, pencils	40 min.	Ch. 6, Les. 2	
	Chronicling the Split	paper, pencils	40 min.	Ch. 6, Les. 3	
Why Character Counts pages 64–65	**Responsibility** Students read about responsibility and complete the follow-up activity.	pencils	45 min.	Ch. 6, Les. 2	
Economic Literacy pages 66–67	**Taxes** Students read about taxes and complete the follow-up activity.	pencils	30 min.	Ch. 6, Les. 2	
Citizenship pages 68–69	**Bill of Rights** Students read about the Bill of Rights, hold a discussion, and complete a writing activity.	pencils	40 min.	Ch. 7, Les. 1	

Planning Options

👤 individual 👥 partners 👥👤 group

	Activity	Materials	🕐	Link	
Drama Activity pages 72–75	**Antigone—An Adaptation** Students read a partial adaptation of this famous play.		30 min.	Ch. 9, Les. 2	👥👤
Simulations and Games pages 76–77	**Fact or Fiction** Students try to decide if statements are fact or fiction.	pencils, index cards, resource materials	40 min.	U4	👥👤
	Word Scramble Students unscramble unit terms.	paper, pencils	40 min.	U4	
	Pop-Up Greeks Students compete with each other to try to answer questions.	index cards, pencils, resource materials	40 min.	U4	
	Debate on Democracy Students stage a mock debate.	resource materials	30 min.	Ch. 9, Les. 1	
Long-Term Project pages 78–79	**A Guidebook to Greek Theater**			Ch. 9, Les. 2	👥👤
	Week 1 Students brainstorm about their portions of the project.	paper, pencils	45 min.		
	Week 2 Students begin writing their mini-reports.	paper, pencils, resource materials	45 min.		
	Week 3 Students design and create their artwork.	craft paper, glue or tape, markers or paints and paintbrushes, construction paper, scissors	45 min.		
	Week 4 Students make a short presentation and show their artwork.	mini-reports, artwork	45 min.		

© Harcourt

	Activity	Materials	🕐	Link	
Short-Term Projects pages 80–81	**Travel to the Cyclades** Students make travel posters.	posterboard, colored pencils or markers, resource materials	40 min.	Ch. 8, Les. 1	
	Answer Like Socrates Students mimic Socrates in a discussion.	paper, pencils	20 min.	Ch. 9, Les. 2	
	The Hippocratic Oath Students research, study, and interpret the modern Hippocratic Oath.	posterboard, markers, resource materials	40 min.	Ch. 9, Les. 2	
	The First Olympics Students make posters for the ancient Olympic Games.	posterboard, markers or paints, paintbrushes, resource materials	40 min.	Ch. 8, Les. 3	
Writing Projects pages 82–83	**A Minoan Web Page**	paper, pencils	30 min.	Ch. 8, Les. 2	
	A Greek Guidebook to Gods and Goddesses	paper, pencils	40 min.	Ch. 8, Les. 2	
	Fashion Your Own Fable	paper, pencils	30 min.	Ch. 8, Les. 4	
	A Letter Home	paper, pencils	30 min.	Ch. 8, Les. 4	
	Agree or Disagree?	paper, pencils	40 min.	Ch. 9, Les. 1	
	History Makers	paper, pencils	30 min.	Ch. 9, Les. 2	
Why Character Counts pages 86–87	**Patriotism** Students read about patriotism and complete the follow-up activity.	pencils	30 min.	Ch. 8, Les. 4	
Economic Literacy pages 88–89	**Supply and Demand** Students read about the laws of supply and demand and complete the follow-up activity.	pencils	30 min.	Ch. 8, Les. 3	
Citizenship pages 90–91	**Equality** Students read about the concept of equality, hold a discussion, and complete a writing activity.	pencils	40 min.	Ch. 8, Les. 4	

UNIT 5 Planning Options

👤 individual **👥 partners** **👥👥 group**

	Activity	Materials	🕐	Link	
Drama Activity pages 94–97	**Conversations in History** Students listen in as significant Indian and Chinese leaders are interviewed.		30 min.	U5	👥👥👥
Simulations and Games pages 98–99	**Make Your Own Word Search** Students create a word search game.	graph paper, pencils	40 min.	U5	👥👥👥
	Describe It! Students use words and gestures to describe important concepts.	stopwatch, index cards, pencils	40 min.	U5	
	How Many Words? Students make as many smaller words as they can from unit terms.	paper, pencils	40 min.	U5	
	City Planners Students plan a city in the Indus River Valley.	paper, pencils, resource materials	30 min.	Ch. 10, Les. 1	
Long-Term Project pages 100–101	**East and West: A Comparative Study**			U5	👥👥👥
	Week 1 Students brainstorm and divide tasks for the project.	paper, pencils	45 min.		
	Week 2 Students begin assembling their displays.	posterboard, glue, scissors, markers, tape, resource materials	45 min.		
	Week 3 Students continue work on their displays.	posterboard, markers, glue, scissors, resource materials	45 min.		
	Week 4 Students make short presentations and show their displays.	completed displays	45 min.		

© Harcourt

	Activity	Materials	🕐	Link	
Short-Term Projects pages 102–103	**Ancient Harappan Seals** Students make ancient seals out of clay.	modeling clay, stylus or pen for marking, string, resource materials	40 min.	Ch. 10, Les. 1	👤
	Exploring the _Bhagavad Gita_ Students interpret lines from the _Bhagavad Gita_.	paper, pencils, resource materials	20 min.	Ch. 10, Les. 2	👥
	An Army of Faces Students draw figures from the terra-cotta army of Shi Huangdi.	drawing paper, colored pencils, resource materials	30 min.	Ch. 11, Les. 3	👤
	Illustrating Confucius Students illustrate proverbs.	drawing paper, markers or colored pencils	40 min.	Ch. 11, Les. 2	👥👥
Writing Projects pages 104–105	**A Farmer's Eye View**	paper, pencils	40 min.	Ch. 10, Les. 1	👤
	Classes and Castes	paper, pencils	40 min.	Ch. 10, Les. 2	
	Comparison Chart of Indian Religions	paper, pencils	40 min.	Ch. 10, Les. 2–4	
	A Turning Point	paper, pencils	30 min.	Ch. 10, Les. 4	
	Think About It	paper, pencils	30 min.	Ch. 11, Les. 3	
	Interpreting Confucius	paper, pencils		Ch. 11, Les. 2	
Why Character Counts pages 108–109	**Caring** Students read about caring and complete the follow-up activity.	pencils	30 min.	Ch.11, Les. 2	👤
Economic Literacy pages 110–111	**Goods and Services** Students read about goods and services and complete the follow-up activity.	pencils	30 min.	U5	👤
Citizenship pages 112–113	**Equal Employment Opportunity** Students read about equal employment opportunity in the United States, hold a discussion, and complete a writing activity.	pencils	40 min.	Ch. 10, Les. 2	👤 👥👥

© Harcourt

UNIT 6 Planning Options

👤 individual 👥 partners 👥👥 group

	Activity	Materials	🕐	Link	
Drama Activity pages 116–119	**Ancient Rome Club** Students enhance their knowledge of ancient Rome.		30 min.	U6	👥👥
Simulations and Games pages 120–121	**Tic-Tac-Toe with a Twist** Students answer questions to compete in tic-tac-toe.	paper, pencils, resource materials	40 min.	U6	👥👥
	Add a Fact! Students compete to see who knows the most about various topics.		40 min.	U6	
	Unit Drawing Game Students makes sketches while teammates try to guess what the pictures represent.	stopwatch, index cards	40 min.	U6	
	The Roman Republic & the American Government Students stage a mock summit meeting to discuss forms of government.	paper, pencils, resource materials	30 min.	Ch. 12, Les. 1–3	
Long-Term Project pages 122–123	**The Questaurant: Reviewing Ancient Rome**			U6	👥👥
	Week 1 Students begin writing questions for their menus.	paper, pens, resource materials	45 min.		
	Week 2 Students sort their questions and design maps.	paper, pens, tablecloth material, colored pencils and markers, resource materials	45 min.		
	Week 3 Students work on their murals and complete their menus.	mural paper, pens, yardsticks, markers or crayons, glue, staplers, resource materials	45 min.		
	Week 4 Students visit neighboring questaurants.	pens, pencils	45 min.		

© Harcourt

	Activity	Materials	🕐	Link	
Short-Term Projects pages 124–125	**Cast of Emperors** Students create a playbill.	pens, paper, glue, magazines, resource materials	40 min.	Ch. 13, Les. 1–2	👤
	Roman Holiday Students design postcards from Rome.	blank postcards, pens, colored pencils or markers, resource materials	30 min.	Ch. 13, Les. 3	👤
	Bread and Circus Students make posters of ancient Roman events.	posterboard, colored pencils or markers, resource materials	30 min.	Ch. 13, Les. 3	👥👥👥
	Gods and Goddesses Students depict Greek and Roman gods and goddesses.	pencils, paper, colored markers, resource materials	40 min.	Ch. 14, Les. 1	👥👥👥
Writing Projects pages 126–127	**The Gracchus Brothers' Reforms**	paper, pencils	40 min.	Ch. 12, Les. 4	👤
	Legend vs. History	paper, pencils	40 min.	U6	
	Point of View	paper, pencils	30 min.	Ch. 13, Les. 1	
	A Plebeian Life	paper, pencils	30 min.	Ch. 12, Les. 2	
	Magazine Feature	paper, pencils	40 min.	Ch. 13, Les. 3	
	Roman Religions	paper, pencils	40 min.	U6	
Why Character Counts pages 130–131	**Trustworthiness** Students read about trustworthiness and complete the follow-up activity.	pencils	30 min.	Ch.12–13	👤
Economic Literacy pages 132–133	**Credit** Students read about credit and complete the follow-up activity.	pencils	30 min.	Ch. 12, Les. 2	👤
Citizenship pages 134–135	**Right to Vote and Seek Office** Students read about the right to vote and seek office in the United States, hold a discussion, and complete a writing activity.	pencils	40 min.	Ch. 12, Les. 2	👤 👥👥👥

Answer Key

Unit 1

Daily Geography (pp. 18–19)
1. Africa
2. They ate more plants, and perhaps more meat, and moved over longer distances.
3. Olduvai Gorge
4. Lake Turkana, Kenya
5. fire
6. Africa
7. food, tools, shelter, and clothing
8. a change in climate
9. by crossing land bridges
10. the Sahara
11. Nelson's Bay Cave
12. the Baltic Sea
13. Abu Hureyra
14. New Mexico
15. Monte Verde
16. the Andes Mountains
17. Asia
18. slash-and-burn farming
19. Jarmo
20. Europe
21. Mehrgarh
22. China
23. Africa
24. southwestern Asia
25. Çatal Hüyük
26. Jericho
27. the Syrian Desert
28. the Mediterranean Sea
29. Mesopotamia
30. Eridu, Kish, Ur, and Uruk

Why Character Counts (pp. 20–21)
1. Students' definitions will vary, but should show a basic understanding of the concept of respect, as described at the top of the page.
2. Scenes of dialogue will vary but should illustrate the basic disagreement and how the characters still show respect for each other.

Economic Literacy (pp. 22–23)
1. Students should explain what they will do with their surplus money and why they chose as they did.

Citizenship (pp. 24–25)
1. Answers will vary. Students may write that, in both cases, what was good for the largest number of people was the leaders' major concern.

2. Answers will vary. Students may write that, unlike today, in early times families were able to pass on governing authority.

Write About It
Answers will vary. Students should support their opinions.

Unit 2

Daily Geography (pp. 40–41)
1. They used the river for food, water, irrigation, and transportation.
2. the Tigris and Euphrates Valley, the Nile Valley, and the Indus Valley
3. canals
4. the Fertile Crescent
5. Mesopotamia
6. a plateau
7. tributaries
8. the Ubaid culture
9. Eridu, Uruk, Kish, and Ur
10. caravans
11. the Euphrates River
12. a flood
13. a ziggurat
14. the Sumerians
15. Akkad
16. north
17. Lower Egypt, Upper Egypt, and Nubia
18. delta
19. the Sinai Peninsula
20. Memphis
21. the Great Pyramid at Giza
22. the Hyksos
23. Nubia
24. the Nile River
25. Kerma
26. Napata
27. Meroë
28. from 270 B.C. to A.D. 350
29. an excellent trade network
30. Greek rulers ordered ports built on the Red Sea. Traders began to use sea routes rather than the overland routes that passed through Meroë.

Why Character Counts (pp. 42–43)

1. Students' definitions will vary but should show a basic understanding of the concept of fairness.
2. Students should propose a solution in which each of the two students is treated fairly.

Economic Literacy (pp. 44–45)

1. Answers will vary, but students should explain a time in the past that they remember doing a cost-benefit analysis for something they wanted to buy. Students should identify the item, as well as their final decision about it.
2. Students should show the logical steps involved in a cost-benefit analysis. They should also write the benefits of both buying the item now and waiting to buy it. Students should explain the factors that influenced their decisions.

Citizenship (pp. 46–47)

1. Answers will vary. Students may write that having three branches of government keeps any one branch from becoming too powerful. They may write that having three branches makes things more complicated. Either view should be supported with examples.
2. Answers will vary. Students may write that in a monarchy one person has too much power over all the people. They may write that leaders should be elected by the people and not born into a royal family.

Write About It

Students should address the question of whether it is fair for the president of the United States to have veto power. They should also explain why some laws are changed and whether they agree with the lawmaking process.

Unit 3

Daily Geography (pp. 62–63)

1. Mesopotamia
2. Canaan
3. the Mediterranean Sea
4. south and then west
5. Africa
6. the Nile River
7. the Exodus
8. the Sinai Peninsula
9. Canaan
10. north
11. Egypt and Mesopotamia
12. Jerusalem
13. the Mediterranean Sea
14. Phoenicia and Egypt
15. the northern Israelite tribes in the kingdom of Israel
16. Israel and Judah
17. Samaria and Jerusalem
18. northern Mesopotamia
19. Samaria
20. the Jordan River
21. Judah
22. The Babylonians forced many Judaeans to live in Babylon.
23. the Persian Empire
24. to reclaim Canaan and to rebuild the Temple
25. the Jewish Diaspora
26. Macedonia
27. Jerusalem and the Temple
28. Jabneh
29. the Romans
30. Christianity and Islam

Why Character Counts (pp. 64–65)

1. Students' definitions will vary but should show a basic understanding of the concept of responsibility.
2. Skits should clearly demonstrate students facing a conflict or situation in which they show responsibility. Skits should show that students understand the meaning of responsibility and can apply the definition to an everyday situation.

Economic Literacy (pp. 66–67)

1. Answers should show evidence that students have considered various ways that tax money could be put to use. Students should then describe uses of tax revenue that they would consider to be unfair.
2. Students should clearly explain their impressions of the United States tax system while addressing the other questions in the prompt. Students should explain whether they feel it is fair to have to pay sales tax.

Citizenship (pp. 68–69)

1. Students should explain what freedom of religion means to them.
2. Students should offer at least two examples of freedom of religion in the United States. They may write that people from different religions may practice openly in the same community or learn about different religions at school.

Write About It

Students may write that freedom of religion was important to the early Jews because their entire culture was closely connected with religion. Often, when the Jews were conquered by foreign powers, they were not allowed to express their religious beliefs. This made the Jews feel oppressed and unhappy.

Unit 4

Daily Geography (pp. 84–85)

1. the Balkan Peninsula
2. A peninsula is a stretch of land that is almost completely surrounded by water.
3. the Mediterranean Sea, the Aegean Sea, and the Ionian Sea
4. Turkey
5. an isthmus
6. mountains
7. Crete
8. olives, grapes, and barley
9. sea travel
10. the Cyclades Islands
11. Phoenician traders
12. the Minoan civilization
13. No one has been able to translate the writing on the tablets.
14. Asia Minor
15. Sparta and Athens
16. the mountains and the seas
17. southern Europe, northern Africa, and Asia Minor
18. in the valley of Olympia
19. It was located on an excellent harbor off the Aegean Sea.
20. Mesopotamia
21. It stretched from India in the east to Egypt in the west. Persia had also gained control over the Greek colonies along the coast of Asia Minor.
22. Sardis
23. Salamis
24. the Parthenon
25. the Long Walls
26. Thebes
27. Athens, Corinth, and Argos
28. north of the Greek city-states on the Balkan Peninsula
29. through Asia Minor, across Egypt, and into the heart of Mesopotamia
30. Alexandria

Why Character Counts (pp. 86–87)

1. Students' definitions will vary but should show a basic understanding of the concept of patriotism.
2. Answers will vary. Students may explain that they express patriotism by saying the pledge, raising the United States flag, and so on.

Economic Literacy (pp. 88–89)

1. Students may cite items such as gas, bread, or milk as items that are usually in high demand. Students may write that the price of gas goes up during the summer months because people are often traveling on vacation then.
2. When the demand for cars is low, cars are usually less expensive. Cars offered for sale at the end of the model year are often less expensive than they are earlier in the year. Often the prices of cars drop just before the newest models are introduced. Special discounts can be offered as incentives to create a higher demand for cars.

Citizenship (pp. 90–91)

1. Students should explain what equality as a United States citizen means to them personally.
2. Students should mention that the previous model of government was based on British royalty, where everyone was not equal. Equality between the sexes was not yet an issue. Given the culture at the time, it made sense to write, "All men are created equal."

Write About It

Solon decided to cancel all debts. He set free Athenians who had sold themselves into slavery. Solon also replaced many of the harsher laws written by Draco with fairer ones. Solon laid the foundation for democracy in Athens. He divided the male citizens into four classes. Even men in the lowest classes were able to participate in lawmaking.

© Harcourt

Unit 5

Daily Geography (pp. 106–107)

1. Pakistan, India, and Bangladesh
2. a large area of land separated from the rest of a continent by geographic features
3. the Himalayas
4. The Arabian Sea lies to the west, and the Indian Ocean lies to the east.
5. the northern plains and the Deccan
6. the Indus River and the Ganges River
7. the Arabian Sea
8. The conditions for agriculture were the best in the Indus River Valley.
9. flooding
10. the Indian Ocean
11. Harappa, Lothal, and Mohenjo-Daro
12. the Hindu Kush mountains
13. Afghanistan, Bangladesh, and Pakistan
14. Kalinga
15. Sri Lanka
16. most of central and northern India
17. the Huang He and the Chang Jiang
18. the Huang He or "Yellow River"
19. the Gobi
20. the Yangtze
21. the Plateau of Tibet
22. dry, treeless grasslands
23. eastern China
24. the Himalayas and the Gobi
25. they were so isolated by geographic barriers
26. the Great Wall of China
27. an army of life-size soldiers made from clay and armed with real weapons
28. Chang'an
29. Buddhism
30. Silk Road

Why Character Counts (pp. 108–109)

1. Students' definitions will vary but should show a basic understanding of the concept of caring.
2. Answers will vary. All questions should be addressed in the essay.

Economic Literacy (pp. 110–111)

1. Students should write that durable goods are much more expensive than nondurable goods, so more careful planning is necessary. Students may write that little planning is necessary to decide to purchase lunch, but to purchase a new bicycle, you would need to save more money.
2. Students should list services and not goods. They may cite trips to the dentist or doctor. To answer the second question, students should explain that when they go to a movie or a baseball game, they are paying the owners of the stadium or theater for the entertainment and the right to use the seats.

Citizenship (pp. 112–113)

1. Students should explain that some issues are important to every person in the nation. Issues of this magnitude are different than local issues. Lawmakers and members of government want to make sure that federal laws protect everybody.
2. Students may explain that, as time passed, more and more specific cases of discrimination that were not specifically covered in Title VII of the Civil Rights Act of 1964 arose; these required that additional laws be made.

Write About It

For the first question, students should explain that the caste system had everything to do with a person's job in ancient India. A person was born into a certain caste and was unable to move out of it. There was no opportunity to choose a profession or social standing. Answers will vary for the second and third questions.

Unit 6

Daily Geography (pp. 128–129)
1. a peninsula
2. the Adriatic Sea, the Mediterranean Sea, and the Tyrrhenian Sea
3. the Apennines
4. volcanoes
5. Erupting volcanoes deposited ash on the peninsula, which greatly enriched the soil, and the climate on the peninsula is mild, which makes for a long growing season.
6. central Europe
7. seven hills south of the Tiber River
8. the Tiber River
9. The Romans defeated the Etruscans from the north, the Samnites from the east, and the Greeks from the south.
10. He crossed the Mediterranean Sea into what is now Spain, then marched over the Alps to Rome.
11. the Alps
12. northern Africa
13. in northern Africa
14. Corinth
15. Pergamum
16. the Mediterranean Sea
17. France
18. the Rubicon River
19. Egypt
20. Africa, Asia, and Europe
21. roads
22. a huge fire
23. Judaea
24. aqueducts
25. a circus
26. the Colosseum
27. temples
28. Judaea, Egypt, Cyprus, and other regions
29. Syria Palaestina
30. Bethlehem

Why Character Counts (pp. 130–131)
1. Students' definitions will vary, but should show a basic understanding of the concept of trustworthiness.
2. Answers will vary. All opinions should be supported.

Economic Literacy (pp. 132–133)
1. Answers will vary. Other types of credit include mortgages and car financing. Students may also mention a personal loan as a type of credit.
2. Answers will vary. Students may recommend setting a spending limit on credit cards, paying off the balance every month, and finding a credit card with the lowest possible interest rate.

Citizenship (pp. 133–134)
1. Answers will vary. Students may focus on the fact that people in some countries are not allowed to vote.
2. Answers will vary.

Write About It
Answers will vary. Students may discuss the corruption that weakened the Roman Republic. Students may also point out that eventually the republic became an empire.